WORLD'S MOST EVIL MEN

THE WORLD'S MOST EVIL MEN

By
Neil Blandford
and
Bruce Jones

HAMLYN

First published in 1985 by Octopus Books Ltd

This edition published in 1994 by
The Hamlyn Publishing Group
an imprint of Reed Consumer Books Ltd
Michelin House, 81 Fulham Road
London SW3 6RB
and Auckland, Melbourne, Singapore and Toronto

ISBN 0 600 58608 1

A CIP catalogue record for this book is available from the British Library

Printed in Great Britain by Cox & Wyman Ltd

Contents

ACKNOWLEDGEMENTS

In a factual book such as this, the authors must draw on many reference works in the course of their research. Some of these are specifically mentioned in the text. But two invaluable books deserve particular acknowledgement and are highly recommended for further reading. They are: *The Directory Of Infamy* by Jonathon Green (Mills & Boon 1980), and *A Criminal History Of Mankind* by Colin Wilson (Granada, 1984). Other authors to whom acknowledgements are due are: Gordon Honeycombe (*The Murders Of The Black Museum* Hutchinson, 1982), David Mitchell (*Pirates* Thames & Hudson, 1976), Dennis Elsenburg, Uri Dan and Ell Landau (*Meyer Lansky: Mogul Of The Mob* Paddington Press, 1979), John Beattie (*Klaus Barbie – His Life And Career* Methuen/Daily Star, 1984) and Herbert Walther (editor of *Hitler* Bison Books, 1978).

The publishers would like to thank the following for their kind permission to reproduce the pictures used in this book:
Keystone Press Agency 13, 24, 37, 103, 111, 112, 124, 144, 149; Topham Picture Library 21, 141, 144, 156, 157, 162; Mary Evans Picture Library 43, 54, 59, 65, 72, 81, 86, 191; Popperfoto 93, 99; Fox Photos 106; Central Press Photos 117.

‘I never wonder to see men wicked but I often wonder to see them not ashamed.’

Jonathan Swift (1711)

Chapter One

TWENTIETH-CENTURY TYRANTS

Regimes whose rule is terror . . . led by men to whom power has meant a licence to corrupt, maim and murder.

'Some men delight in things for no other reason but because they are ugly and infamous.'

Samuel Butler (1680)

Idi Amin

The dimming of the street lights on the warm, tropical nights in Kampala was always an accurate barometer of the morale of the people of Uganda.

Privileged visitors, arms salesmen and foreign diplomats in the two showpiece hotels would grumble loudly when the cocktail bars were plunged into darkness and the elevators jammed between floors.

But the uncomplaining residents of Kampala would leave the unlit cinemas and cheap little coffee shops in fearful silence to go home and spend a sleepless night behind barricaded doors.

Fitful blackouts in the power supply were a sign that Uganda's President Idi Amin had just completed another busy day of butchery. The drop in the voltage usually meant only one thing . . .

That the hydro-electric generators at Owen Falls Dam, 40 miles west of Kampala, were once again clogged with rotting corpses.

Despite the constant boat patrols on Lake Victoria, the source of the waters of the Nile, the maintenance engineers couldn't hope to spot every dead body swept by the currents towards their filter grids. They had allies helping them to scavenge the lake clear of the harvest of murder victims: the teeming colonies of crocodiles. But even these voracious reptiles became bloated and lazy. The pickings were too rich for them.

Time after time the generators had to be shut down and the water inlets cleared of that day's toll of death, usually 40 or 50 bodies in a 24-hour period.

In eight years of ruling his country in a torrent of blood and terror, Idi Amin had 500,000 of his fellow Ugandans ruthlessly and systematically butchered. He ordered the grisly mutilation of one of his own wives. He killed crusading clergymen, nosy journalists, his own diplomats and a helpless, frail elderly hijack hostage. He even tasted the flesh of some of his victims in cannibal ritual.

He killed political opponents, real and imagined, to stay in power. And he killed countless ordinary men and women for profit, sometimes for the sake of a few hundred pounds.

He personally supervised the actions of Uganda's 'State Research Bureau', an organisation which was a cross between the Gestapo and Murder Incorporated, dealing in state-sponsored torture, contract killing, drug running and currency smuggling.

For almost a hundred years, the fertile land of Uganda had been part of the

British Empire, 'The Pearl of Africa' according to its colonial administrators. Spread over the hills and valleys of a high plateau, its gentle climate makes it a pleasant garden nudging the Equator. It had enormous strategic value but when the 'wind of change' blew through Africa, the pressure for independence for Uganda became irresistible.

An astute lawyer and professional politician, Milton Obote became the first Prime minister when he triumphed in the hastily organized elections in 1962. His first priority was to forge some sort of unity among the 14 million Ugandans who owed more allegiance to their tribal chiefs than to any government in Kampala.

The ruling edicts of some of the chiefs of the 40 different tribes of Uganda often seemed to carry more authority than the decisions of any ballot-box Government. Mindful of this, Obote, a member of the minority Langi tribe, appointed the powerful ruler of the Buganda tribe, King Freddy, as President of Uganda. The Buganda tribe, largely Anglicized by colonial commissioners and missionaries, were the largest single tribal group. They considered themselves an elite.

But in placating them, Milton Obote earned himself the growing distrust of all the other tribes. Shortly after independence, however, he began slowly to reduce the powers of King Freddy.

By 1966 Buganda tribesmen were agitating more and more violently for Obote's overthrow. He needed to pit some military muscle against them and chose the deputy commander of the army, Idi Amin.

Amin had all the qualifications. He was an outsider, a Kakwa tribesman from the furthest flung province of Uganda, bordering Sudan. He was a Moslem who spoke virtually no English and was only semi-literate. He wouldn't be loath to dish out some rough justice to the Bugandans.

A former sergeant in the King's African Rifles, Amin was the ex-heavyweight-boxing champion of Uganda, a hulk of a man who, at six feet four inches tall and weighing more than twenty stone, easily dominated his fellow Ugandan Army staff officers.

His British commanding officer before independence had enthusiastically earmarked Amin as 'a tremendous chap to have around.' And though he was tough and swaggering, he was slow-witted and had never shown even the slightest tendency to try to grasp the complexities of politics.

Amin responded swiftly and energetically to the task the Prime Minister had given him. Using a 122mm gun mounted on his personal Jeep, he blew gaping holes in King Freddie's Palace. The Bugandan leader, warned of the danger just before the attack, fled into hiding and eventually made his way to Britain where he died in lonely exile.

For the next four years, Idi Amin was the Prime Minister's trusted strong arm man. Milton Obote was calm and relaxed when he flew off to Singapore in January 1971 to attend a Commonwealth Conference. He was about to fly home to Uganda when he heard the news on the radio . . . Idi Amin had just mobilized the Army and declared himself the country's new ruler.

The overgrown village bully turned military chief had decided that if he was to do the dirty work in Uganda he might just as well install himself as its supreme authority.

Milton Obote went into exile having learned an embarrassing political lesson. For the people of Uganda, cautiously celebrating his overthrow, the experience was to be painful to the point of torture and death.

Amin's first move was to pacify tribal enemies and buy valuable breathing space. He persuaded Buganda leaders that he himself had actually tipped off King Freddy and given him time to flee to safety. He arranged for the release of many political prisoners detained by Obote and had the body of the dead tribal King flown back from Britain for a ceremonial burial.

Amin was deeply affected by the ritual outpouring and lavish expense of the Buganda tribesmen at the burial ceremony. The experience was to be put to hideous use later.

Amin then moved against the most potent potential threat to his new power – the officers of the Ugandan Army.

He announced a new programme of army re-structuring and began by ordering 36 senior officers, Langi and Acholi tribesmen, to report to Makindye Prison for training in internal security. Disgruntled, but seduced by the thought of forming part of a government of military men instead of politicians, the officers arrived at Makindye. They were locked in cells and bayonetted to death.

The former army chief-of-staff, Brigadier Suleiman Hussein, was arrested and taken to yet another prison where he was beaten to death with rifle butts. His head was severed and taken to Amin's new palatial home in Kampala where the president preserved it in the freezer compartment of his refrigerator.

In two widely separated army barracks, at Mbarara and Jinja, the elite of the officer corps were lined up on the parade ground to take a salute from an armoured column. The tanks swept across the square, swung into line abreast formation and crushed most of the officers to death. Those left alive were used for target practice by riflemen. At another barracks, the remaining staff officers were herded into a briefing room for a lecture by Amin. As they saw his gleaming black Mercedes sweep into the square, the doors were locked from outside and grenades were lobbed through the windows.

Within five months Amin had killed most of the trained professional officers in his army. Yet the news was kept secret from the Ugandan people, who were simply told that a few disloyal officers had been court-martialled and executed. To make up the gaps in the ranks, Amin promoted fellow Kakwa tribesmen. Cooks and drivers, mess orderlies and wireless operators became majors and colonels overnight.

Idi Amin, one-time Life President of Uganda

But the word of the massacres had filtered out to two inquiring Americans, Nicholas Stroh, son of a wealthy Detroit brewer and a former writer for the *Philadelphia Bulletin* newspaper, was working as a freelance journalist in Africa. He joined forces with another American, Robert Siedle, a sociologist at Makere University in Kampala, to start asking questions about the army massacres.

At Mbarara barracks they were granted an interview with the new commander, Major Juma Aiga, a former taxi driver who had won an instant army commission. When their persistent questioning became too much, Major Aiga telephoned President Amin. His reply was terse: 'Kill them'.

Both men were gunned down on the spot and a few days later Aiga was openly driving around Kampala in Stroh's Volkswagen car. When the American Embassy demanded an investigation into the disappearance of the two men, they got nowhere.

As Amin went off on his first foreign trip as a head of government, he had already broken the backbone of the Ugandan Army. He was all-powerful, but he returned from his journeys to Israel and Britain empty-handed. His outright demands to both countries for millions of pounds in cash donations were refused. And the word went round the tight community of international diplomacy that the new president was not just a stupid, arrogant man. He was mad and dangerous.

Within a year Uganda was bankrupt. Amin's reaction was to order the Bank of Uganda to print millions of worthless banknotes to pump into the economy. All that remained of the reserves of U.S. dollars and sterling were made available for his personal use.

In Kampala the price of a bar of soap rose to £6, two weeks' wages for the average worker on the coffee plantations which were among the country's few sources of income.

Temporary salvation was offered by one other extravagant dictator, Libya's Colonel Ghadaffi. The price was one Amin was only too happy to pay for their newly formed alliance. As Libyan money poured into Kampala to keep the country barely afloat, Amin kept his side of the bargain. He ranted and raved against the State of Israel and kicked out the small group of skilled Israeli engineers employed on the construction projects which formed Israel's limited aid to Uganda.

Angered and hurt, the Israelis pulled out with their bulldozers and a meticulous mass of paperwork and blueprints. The documents included one slim volume which was later to help make history – the plans of Israel's last gift to Uganda, the new passenger terminal, control tower and runway layout of Entebbe Airport.

Amin, anxious to prove to Ghadaffi that he was a worthy protégé, opened an office in Kampala for the Palestine Liberation Organization with full diplomatic status. He capped it by pronouncing his admiration for his political hero, Adolf Hitler. As Amin drew up plans for a memorial to Hitler in the centre of Kampala, the world began to realize that some awful disaster was beginning to unfold.

They didn't have long to wait.

The Libyan money was barely propping up Uganda, and now Amin had hundreds of his chosen henchmen on the payroll of his new police force, The State Research Bureau. He bought their loyalty with lavish gifts of money and expensive cars, luxuries like video tape recorders and whisky and clothes imported from London and Paris.

One hot August night in 1972, dinner guests at Amin's palace, State House in Entebbe, were shocked and revolted when he left the table and returned from the kitchen with the frost-encrusted head of Brigadier Hussein from the freezer. In a ranting fit of rage Amin screamed abuse at the severed head, heaving cutlery at it, then ordered his guests to leave.

Two nights later he turned up unexpectedly in eastern Uganda and announced that God had appeared to him and told him that Uganda's population of 50,000 Asians, mainly tradesmen and merchants, doctors and nurses, were causing all Uganda's economic problems. He ordered them to leave the country within 90 days.

For the next three months Amin's voice could be heard on Uganda radio, making a daily count down to his deadline. Although most of the Asians had lived in Uganda for generations, forming the backbone of the nation's commerce, they fled in terror leaving behind their homes, offices, shops and plantations.

In November that year, Amin gave away the choice businesses to his friends and cronies. Pharmacies and surgeries were handed over to motor mechanics from the State Research Bureau, textile warehouses were given to Research Bureau telephone operators and army corporals. Within weeks the shops were deserted, their stocks sold and the shelves never filled again . . . and the men of the State Research Bureau wanted to be paid again.

With no money or property left to meet their demands, Amin gave them the only asset he had left, the lives of his fellow Ugandans.

It was the most bestial mass murder contract in history. Amin gave his bureau torturers the licence to kill for profit.

He knew the tradition of Ugandans, their deep reverence for the last remains of dead relatives and how they will spend every last Ugandan shilling of their money and part with anything of value to recover the body of a loved one for burial. In many of the tribes 'body finders' will earn their rewards by tracking through the bush to find the body of some father or son who has died in some remote cattle grazing area or drowned in the fast flowing waters of the Nile.

The State Research Bureau became the killers – and the body finders.

Cruising through the street of Kampala in their imported cars, wearing their 'uniform' of gaudy silk shirts and bell bottom trousers, they openly arrested ordinary townspeople. And at their headquarters, only a few hundred yards from Amin's palatial home, they ruthlessly butchered their victims.

As the corpses piled up in the basement cells of the three storey building, other Research Bureau jailers were despatched to tell grieving families that their loved ones had disappeared after being arrested and were feared dead. For a body finding fee of £150, or every last possession the family owned, the State Research murderers drove the widows and weeping sons and daughters to a lush forest on the outskirts of Kampala.

Almost every gulley and bush concealed a dead body. Many nights as many as a hundred families made the grisly trip. The bodies not reclaimed were thrown into Lake Victoria, useless assets written off as a 'business' loss until they floated through the sluced gates of the Owens Falls Dam and the hydro-electric generators.

But the executions by firing squads at the Research Bureau became a problem. The neighbouring French Embassy staff complained directly to Amin about the constant gunfire throughout the night. Amin, sinking deeper and deeper into depravity, discussed a solution with the head of the Bureau, Lieutenant Isaac Malyamungu.

Malyamungu, a gatekeeper at a textile factory before Amin made him a government official, was a notoriously sadistic killer. Before executing the mayor of the provincial town of Masaka, he had paraded the badly mutilated man through the streets carrying his own amputated genitals in his hands. Now he and Amin calmly came up with the answer to the problem of maintaining the horrendous flow of lucrative killings without the disturbing, continuous rattle of gunfire. The murder victim would be kept alone in the basement, while another prisoner was offered the promise of reprieve if he would batter the solitary man to death with a 16lb sledgehammer.

Terrified and pleading for their lives, few prisoners were brave enough to refuse the offer. But once they had carried out their sickening task, the roles were changed. The unwilling executioner, usually sobbing and demented, would be left alone. He would become the solitary man, while in the cell next door another Ugandan was being given the sledgehammer and the heartless promise of life if he would repeat the procedure.

Even as the death toll rose, Amin still found time to indulge in personal episodes of unbelievable horror.

In March 1974 he went through a simple Moslem ritual to divorce three of his four wives. He accused them of meddling in his affairs and ordered them out of his home. Three months later one of the young ex-wives, Kay Amin, died in an apartment in Kampala as the result of a clumsy abortion attempt. She had been four months pregnant. Amin, in a state of fury, rushed to the mortuary to see her body. A few minutes later, quiet and unemotional, he gave a series of orders to the hospital surgeons and then left.

Two hours later he returned and satisfied himself that his orders had been carried out. Then he strode into the hospital morgue with his most junior wife, Sarah, and six-year-old Aliga Amin, the young son of Kay.

'Pay close attention to what you see,' he roared at them. 'Kay was a wicked woman, now look at what has become of her.'

Kay Amin's mutilated torso lay on the operating table. Her head and all her limbs had been amputated. Now her head had been reversed and sewn back on face down on her torso. Her legs had been neatly sutured on to her shoulders and her arms attached firmly to her bloodstained pelvis.

The swaggering arrogance of Idi Amin came to an end on 4 July 1976 although his brutality was to continue for almost another three years.

On 28 June an Air France airliner hijacked by a team of Palestinians arrived at Entebbe Airport. The plane had been en route from Tel Aviv to Paris when it had been commandeered shortly after a stop-over in Athens. It carried some 300 passengers.

In the heart of an African country governed by a Hitler-worshipper, far from any hope of rescue, the Palestinians confidently drew up their demands while Amin looked on, gloating and basking in the world limelight.

Amin helped to draft the blackmail demand that all the passengers would be killed in 48 hours if 53 Palestinian prisoners in jail in Israel and Europe were not released. As international tension mounted, the deadline was extended until the early hours of July 4, and passengers who were not Jewish were allowed to go.

Two days before the deadline, as the terrified hostages were huddled in the passenger terminal, one elderly Londoner, Dora Bloch, who held dual British-Israeli nationality, choked on a piece of food and was driven 20 miles from the airport to hospital in Kampala.

But as Idi Amin was being seen world-wide on television, badgering the hostages in the passenger lounge, the Israeli engineers in Tel Aviv unlocked a filing cabinet and began to pore over the vital blueprints of the airport they had helped to build.

Up and down the east coast of Africa an incredible international humanitarian conspiracy began to take shape. Shortly after midnight on 3 July, a task force of Israeli Air Force planes filled with commandoes came swooping over Lake Victoria. In silent co-operation they had been allowed to refuel and fly through the radar screens of Kenya, Uganda's neighbour.

The Israeli planes, guided by their own blueprints, landed swiftly and taxied to the precise spot in the terminal buildings where the hostages were being held. In less than an hour they took off again with the rescued hostages, leaving behind 20 of Idi Amin's troops dead and the seven hijackers killed on the spot. They also took with them the bodies of two of their own men caught in the crossfire.

But elderly Dora Bloch remained behind in hospital in Kampala, frail and barely able to breathe. Amin decided to vent his fury on her.

Sixteen hours after the Entebbe rescue mission, British High Commissioner Peter Chandley was allowed to visit Mrs Bloch. He tried to reassure the frightened woman and left the hospital briefly to prepare some food for her.

Shortly after he left, two State Research Bureau officials crashed through the doors of the hospital ward. They pistol-whipped the frail widow and dragged her down three flights of steps. Half an hour later they dumped her bullet-riddled body in a field on the outskirts of Kampala.

When the High Commissioner returned to the hospital, Amin simply announced that Mrs Bloch had gone the day before, returned to the airport under escort before the Entebbe Raid.

Idi Amin's last desperate mad gamble to hold the reins of power collapsed in April 1979. To scare the Ugandan people into submission, he claimed that the country was threatened by bloody invasion from its southern neighbour, Tanzania.

To give substance to his fantasies, he ordered small contingents of his troops across the Tanzanian border on raids against the 'invaders'. Such provocation was too much for Tanzanian President Julius Nyrere. His soldiers repelled the attacks and then drove deep into Uganda. They were welcomed with open arms by the long-suffering Ugandans as they advanced swiftly towards Kampala.

In one final broadcast, Idi Amin urged his troops to join him in a last stand at the town of Jinja, near the Owens Falls Dam. The soldiers didn't turn up. But then neither did Idi Amin. He had fled in his personal aircraft to the safety of Libya to seek sanctuary with his ally, Colonel Ghadaffi.

Five years after his overthrow, Idi Amin was still safely living in luxury in a private suite of an hotel in Saudi Arabia, the guest of the Moslem royal rulers of that country.

He would still rant about his return to Uganda and his self-appointed role in international politics. But this time no one was listening.

Prime Minister Milton Obote was back in power in Kampala. The country still suffered the ravages of the long years of Amin's tyranny. But the power supply flowed smoothly from the Owens Falls Dam hydro-electric generators, and the crocodiles in Lake Victoria had only the birds' nests in the swamps to prey on for a decent meal.

Pol Pot

He has a broad, chubby face with sparkling, grandfatherly eyes and thick lips which split into a toothy, genial grin. He looks slightly comical, an impression not dispelled by his peculiar name, Pol Pot. But there is nothing funny about Pol Pot . . . he is a tyrannical fanatic responsible for the coldly calculated extermination of three million people.

Pol Pot spent just four years on the world stage, as the shadowy leader of Kampuchea (formerly Cambodia) after the overthrow of President Lon Nol in 1975. Yet in that short period he virtually destroyed a nation – all for the sake of an unworkable creed that he imposed unyieldingly on a starving and terrorized population. Under his rule, a once-beautiful country became known as 'The Land of the Walking Dead'.

Little is known of Pol Pot's background, and what is known could easily have been the invention of his propaganda machine. It is said that he was brought up in a peasant community in Cambodia's Kampong Thom province and was educated at a Buddhist temple where, for two years, he was a monk. In the 1950s he won a scholarship to study electronics in Paris where, like so many other students at the time, he found it fashionable to espouse left-wing causes.

Also in Paris in the 1950s was another left-wing Cambodian student, Khieu Samphan, who used his political science courses to formulate an extraordinary philosophy of rural revolution. His theory was that to rid itself of the vestiges of colonial rule and to avoid capitalist exploitation, Cambodia must regress to a peasant economy – without towns, without industry, without currency, without education.

It is unlikely that Pol Pot and Khieu Samphan ever met in Paris. But back among the Khmer people of Cambodia, they teamed up and set about making Khieu's crackpot creed come true, using as their instrument the newly-formed and Chinese-backed Communist Party of Kampuchea.

After a decade of political intrigue and rural guerrilla warfare, in 1975 the communists finally overthrew President Lon Nol and became masters of the capital, Phnom Penh. By now the party was known as the Khmer Rouge. Khieu Samphan became its figurehead. But the real power lay in the hands of the former peasant from the provinces, Prime Minister Pol Pot. And he immediately put political daydreams into horrific, brutal, uncompromising reality.

The capital was emptied. As many as three million of its citizens were stripped of all they possessed and were ordered out of their homes. Irrespective of whether they were old, sick, pregnant, crippled, newly born or dying, they were marched into the countryside and herded into vast communes of as many as 10,000. No town was left inhabited. Even villages were emptied of their people. Everybody had to work in the fields.

Of course, not everyone could. The aged and the ill died of exhaustion. The young died of starvation. And the crippled and the lame were clubbed to death.

Living in malaria-ridden swamps, with no proper shelter or sanitation, the new 'peasants' were frogmarched into the paddy fields to work a minimum of eleven hours a day. They were fed a daily bowl of gruel and a morsel of dried fish. They worked nine days on and one day off . . . but that tenth day of rest was taken up with political indoctrination. Children began their working lives at the age of seven.

Not only did the Khmer Rouge abolish towns and communities, they abolished families, husbands and wives being split up and placed in different co-operatives. They also abolished personal property, apart from the one sleeping mat and one pair of black overalls handed out no more than once a year. Since there was no property and no trade, there was no need for money, so they abolished that too.

Because there was no education apart from political indoctrination, Pol Pot abolished the schools and colleges. All books were burned. With education thereby shown to be non-essential, he abolished the educated classes – and had them murdered by the tens of thousands. Also eliminated, by bayonet or pickaxe, were priests, political reactionaries, prison inmates and the defeated soldiers of ex-president Lon Nol.

Anyone who complained, or even questioned the system, would be instantly executed by clubbing. Special offenders, like those starving peasants found cannibalizing dead bodies, would be buried up to their heads in the ground and left to die. Their heads would then be cut off and stuck on stakes as a warning to others.

The extermination continued for four years, with no hope of help from the outside world. Refugees reaching neighbouring countries told stories of horrors that were unbelievable. Yet, with no diplomatic ties, no travel, not even a postal service, the renamed nation of Kampuchea was an impenetrable armed camp seemingly set on the genocide of its own people.

The world's repugnance was unheeded; protest appeared futile. In March 1978, Britain reported Kampuchea to the United Nations Commission On Human Rights. The Khmer Rouge's embassy in Peking issued an hysterical response, saying: 'The British imperialists have no right to speak of the rights of man. The world knows well their barbarous and abject nature. Britain's leaders are living in opulence on top of a pile of rotting corpses while the proletariat have only the right to be unemployed, to steal and to become prostitutes.' There was

A grim scene in the Museum of Genocidal Crime outside Phnom Penh

little chance of a reasoned debate . . . and indeed Pol Pot's ministers sent their regrets that they could find no one with the time to spare to attend the United Nations human rights hearings.

Predictably, it was military might, not moral right, that brought the overthrow of Pol Pot and his murderous henchmen. Vietnam signed a pact with Kampuchea's only ally, China, and in 1978 Vietnamese forces which had been skirmishing with the Khmer Rouge for years launched a full-scale invasion. The Chinese did not step in to aid Pol Pot, and in January 1979 his regime fell to the invading Vietnamese. So swift was his overthrow that the chubby little despot had to flee from Phnom Penh in a white Mercedes limousine only two hours before the first of Hanoi's troops arrived.

Pol Pot fought on from his power base among his dedicated followers in the countryside. He formed the Khmer People's National Liberation Front and announced a hypocritical manifesto promising political and religious freedom. Khieu Samphan remained titular head of the Khmer Rouge. In a rare interview with foreign journalists in 1980, he said the mistakes made by his regime were mainly in implementation of policy. For instance, he said, over-zealous commune leaders had often forgotten to give workers their one day off in ten. And as for the massacres, he said: 'To talk about systematic murder is odious. If we had really killed at that rate, we would have no one to fight the Vietnamese.'

No one will ever know the truth about how many Khmers died of disease, starvation, neglect, brutalization, murder or massacre. But in June 1979, Foreign Minister Ieng Sary admitted to three million deaths since the Khmer Rouge came to power. As there were only eight million Khmers in the pre-revolutionary census, it was pointed out by journalists that this did not seem a good record for a four-year-old government. The Minister was apologetic. He had an explanation, he said. The orders from Pol Pot had been 'misunderstood.' The massacres had, he said, been 'a mistake'.

'Emperor' Bokassa

For a brief period just before the 'coronation' of self-styled Emperor Jean Bedel Bokassa it seemed as if some glimmer of humanity might be creeping into his tyrannical madness. Important diplomats and influential international businessmen from many parts of the world were preparing to attend his spectacular enthronement ceremony in Bangui, capital of the land-locked Central African Republic, the sprawling former French colony in the heart of the continent.

At the beginning of December 1977, as rehearsals began for the great event, Bokassa had locked himself away in his palace 50 miles outside the capital watching endless re-runs of a film which had been specially flown to him from London. The film showed the majesty and splendour of the Coronation of Britain's Queen Elizabeth. Bokassa, a violent, squat, ugly little man, seemed to be genuinely moved by the scenes of the splendid pageantry and the spontaneous, heart-felt joy and devotion of the Queen's loyal subjects.

His own coronation, he decided, would be a similarly historic occasion. Even if he couldn't hope to win the hearts of the people he ruled, at least his guests couldn't fail to be impressed. Apparently on a whim, he ordered the governor of Bangui Prison to select a dozen prisoners for more humane treatment. They were to be moved to less cramped cells, given better food than the other inmates and allowed some fresh air in the prison yard. Some prison guards even talked excitedly of a partial amnesty to celebrate the coronation. The prisoners, Bokassa promised, wouldn't be in jail much longer.

Then Bokassa busied himself again supervising the last-minute preparations for the ceremony. The Government of France, headed by his frequent holiday guest, President Valéry Giscard D'Estaing, had generously provided him with credit of £1 million to buy a fleet of Mercedes limousines for his guests and to equip their ceremonial escort with 200 new BMW motorcycles.

It mattered little to the 58-year-old dictator that his country ranked as one of the poorest in the world, with barely ten per cent of the two million population able to read and write and more than a quarter of their children dying of disease and malnutrition before they reached their first birthday.

He planned to spend £10 million in a 48-hour spectacular binge, a regal extravaganza to rival the coronation of his 'hero', the Emperor Napoleon. President Bokassa himself would assume the title Emperor Bokassa and his bankrupt country would be grandly re-named The Central African Empire.

Many political leaders had no stomach for his lunacy and returned their gold-lettered invitation cards with scant apologies for their absence. Even the formally polite British Foreign Office were blunt and rude when they refused to attend. American President Jimmy Carter, outraged by Bokassa's insane claim to Napoleonic grandeur, promptly responded by cutting off all aid to the country.

Bokassa was unrepentant. His rag-tag army formed most of the unenthusiastic onlookers at the triumphal parade through Bangui where the new Emperor would ride in a gilded carriage drawn by eight white horses along the city's only two miles of paved road.

The coronation went ahead with all the panoply of crowns and ermine robes in the sweltering African heat, and the guests were treated to a mouth-watering imperial banquet in Bokassa's palace at Berengo.

Protected by screens of bullet-proof glass in a landscaped garden amid fountains and ornate ivory carvings, they were pampered by uniformed servants who brought them elaborately cooked delicacies served on gold and white porcelain dishes specially imported from the workshops of the master designer, Berardaud of Limoges.

Some of the French and African diplomats, and the Italian and German businessmen, seemed ill at ease in the absurd splendour of their bizarre surroundings. They would have felt distinctly more queasy if they had realized the origins of some of the tastiest morsels served up to them on the Limoges porcelain.

Bokassa had kept his promise to the prison governor. The inmates who had been given food, fresh air and exercise had found their new privileges short-lived. As soon as they had been restored to near normal health, they had been killed, expertly butchered and served up to the unsuspecting guests at Bokassa's celebration feast.

His obsession with the trappings of the power and grace of the age of Napoleon were flattering to many of his French VIP visitors. At least most of them found his mania for all things French to be understandable. His character had been moulded by his long years as a soldier in the French colonial army, where all new

The Coronation of Emperor Bokassa, 28 December, 1977

recruits were thoroughly indoctrinated in the glories of French history and the awesome achievements of its finest soldier, Napoleon Bonaparte.

In 1960, when the French gave independence to the republic, an area almost as large as France itself, most of them were glad to be rid of the task of governing its vast, arid waste. There was some embarassed amusement in 1966 when Colonel Bokassa seized power in a coup from the Republic's civilian government and began to boast of his devotion to France. He swore undying loyalty to French President Charles De Gaulle, whom he lovingly called 'Papa'. The French Government responded with generous aid in return for some minor business concessions and a military foothold in a strategic part of Africa.

In 1975, the new French President Valéry Giscard D'Estaing took advantage of Bokassa's welcome to make several big-game hunting trips to his private game reserve, an area covering most of the eastern half of the country.

There were reports that Bokassa was never slow to shower his visitors with lavish gifts, including fistfuls of diamonds, one of his country's few precious resources, which should have gone to help alleviate the crushing poverty of its people.

By the time Bokassa was in the full grip of his 'imperial' mania, the soaring price of oil had made the country's only other asset, uranium deposits, look like a promising commercial prospect for French developers. Wary of growing evidence of Bokassa's brutality, the French uneasily indulged his regal fantasies while keeping a discreet eye on his appetite for power and showmanship. Within two years of the ludicrous coronation, he had become more than a posturing embarrassment to Paris. He was a bloodthirsty, dangerous liability.

Apparently determined to transform his dusty capital city into a model of French 'provincial' fashion, Bokassa ordered the barefoot schoolchildren of Bangui's only high school to buy expensively tailored school uniforms to be worn at all lessons. Their parents could hardly afford to buy the text books their children needed if they were to have even a basic education. And it hadn't passed unnoticed that the Emperor owned the only clothing factory which produced the school uniforms. It was yet another impossible order from the Emperor which they couldn't obey even if they wanted to. No one foresaw the consequences.

President Bokassa, who had seen his demands for national opera, ballet and art societies dismissed by his weary people, had at one time seemingly grown accustomed to being ignored. But *Emperor* Bokassa, the Napoleon-worshipper, expected every order to be carried out without question.

Two hundred ragged schoolchildren were rounded up by the 'Imperial Guard'. Bokassa gathered them in the yard of Bangui Prison, swaggering among them with his gold-topped cane, bullying the overawed, frightened pupils. 'You will not need school uniforms as long as you stay in prison,' the Empe or screamed at them. Under the threatening guns of the guards, the children were herded into the already overcrowded cells.

Over the next few weeks the killings began. One by one the children were led from the cells for 'school uniform inspection' . . . and mercilessly beaten to death.

News of the mass murders finally reached the disbelieving ears of officials of the French Embassy in Bangui. At first they couldn't bring themselves to accept the evidence. But witness after witness from the prison repeated the same story. And Paris finally woke up to the fact that Jean Bedel Bokassa was more than a comic opera Emperor with his crown and robes and sceptre. He was a monster.

For the honour of France, for the sake of common decency, the Emperor had to go.

The opportunity came a month later when the demented Emperor left Bangui for a visit to another dictator, Colonel Ghadaffi of Libya. As Bokassa stepped off his plane in Tripoli, he learned a lesson in the true French art of power politics and military muscle which would have delighted his long dead hero Napoleon.

At his home in Paris where he had lived since being ousted by Bokassa, African politician David Dacko was roughly shaken awake by French Secret Service agents and given a prepared speech to rehearse and memorize before being bundled into a waiting car. Ten hours later he stumbled from a French military jet at Bangui and asked the French Foreign Legion troops who landed immediately after him to help him to a 'spontaneous' humanitarian overthrow of the evil Bokassa.

Within 24 hours the 'Empire' was effectively back under French control. The deposed Emperor went into exile from Libya to the Ivory Coast in West Africa and then to a run-down château in an unfashionable Paris suburb.

The hardened Legionnaires who searched the grounds of the prison had the grim task of uncovering the mass grave which held the bodies of the dead schoolchildren.

Later, when they stormed the Emperor's Napoleonic palace, they found the bones of another 37 children lying on the tiled floor of the Olympic standard swimming pool. Lounging by the poolside were the predators who had enjoyed the grisly feast, Bokassa's four pet crocodiles. And in the cold storage rooms of the palace kitchens, they found the half-eaten remains of another dozen unnamed victims who had been served up at the Emperor's dining table only the week before.

As the uniform-obsessed Emperor began a new career in exile as a supplier of khaki safari suits to African tourist boutiques, President Giscard D'Estaing announced in Paris that he had sent a personal cheque for £10,000, the value of the diamonds given to him as gifts, to a charity school for children in Bangui.

Papa Doc

Many tyrants have held power over nations by preying on simple human emotions, like fear of invasion by hostile neighbours or by nationalistic pride in conquest over weaker countries. Others have kept themselves in government by rigged elections or by armed suppression of their own downtrodden populations.

But only one modern dictator has ever managed to keep his people enslaved by a grisly combination of machine-gun and mysticism, by the force of a vicious police state and an unholy alliance with the Devil himself and his legions of demons and ghosts, vampires and zombies.

In the era that saw astronauts land on the moon and orbiting laboratories in space, President 'Papa Doc' Duvalier still ruled the republic of Haiti by bullets and black magic, by real live bogeymen who carried very real automatic pistols and by a supernatural 'police force' of living skeletons raised from the dead. Millions of Haitians who suffered the terrors of his 15 years of brutal dictatorship are convinced that he still reigns from beyond the grave, controlling his country's destiny from within the gates of Hell.

The bitter irony of the plight of the 5 million inhabitants of Haiti is that their struggling nation was once hailed as the most progressive in the Caribbean, a proud democracy which showed the way for other countries to free themselves from exploiters and foreign rule.

Haiti shares the island of Hispaniola with the Dominican Republic, and its lush and rolling sub-tropical forests were one of the wondrous sights of the New World for explorer Christopher Columbus when his ship foundered and was wrecked there in December 1492. It was an inauspicious start for a new nation. And over the centuries the people of that island have paid a terrible price for its accidental introduction to the adventurers from the Old World.

By the end of the 16th century most of the original population of Arawak Indians had been wiped out. Many fell victim to newly introduced European diseases. The survivors were literally worked to death on the plantations of their new Spanish masters. When the Spaniards moved on, there was little left to plunder for the next occupants, the rapacious pirates who used Hispaniola as their base for marauding, murder and looting. The buccaneers who controlled the whole western part of the island renamed their territory by its original Indian name – Haiti.

They were soon ousted by a new set of colonial rulers, the French, who revived the plantation system and peopled Haiti with black slaves captured on the west coast of Africa and packed into stinking hulks for the voyage to their new 'home'. The wretched slaves brought with them only two possessions – hatred of their new oppressors and their age-old belief in African witchcraft and demons. The first of these two emotions was to lead to uprisings so passionate and violent that even the all-conquering Emperor Napoleon eventually had to concede defeat in 1804 and Haiti, with its short history of bloodshed and superstition, became the first independent black-governed republic in the world.

Over the years this unhappy land lurched from one incompetent or greedy regime to another. From 1915 to 1934 it was occupied by US Marines. There followed a string of provincial presidents, mostly mulatto descendants of mixed French-negro marriages, each being toppled in the midst of scandal and crisis which only made the already poverty-stricken population more miserable.

But in 1957 a popular new president emerged: François Duvalier, known to his friends and foes alike as 'Papa Doc'. Duvalier was a trained doctor, working on a US medical aid scheme before he turned to politics. Since they provided almost the only source of income for Haiti, the Americans were pleased to see a modern man of medicine as the new ruler. But the black peasants who formed 95 per cent of the population welcomed him for a totally different reason.

To them Duvalier was not so much a doctor, more a medicine man and a pure descendant of African slaves. They were enthralled by his open boast that he was a skilled witch doctor with experience in the dark practices of their voodoo religion, a mixture of French-inspired Christianity and ancient African superstitions. Papa Doc promised that by witchcraft and black magic ritual he would summon the Devil himself to share his power with all the voodoo worshippers of Haiti. On a more practical note, to placate the more educated political opposition, he vowed that the millions of dollars in American aid would be used to raise living standards. At that time, only 10 per cent of the population were literate, the national income averaged £1 a week, and most Haitians died of malnutrition and disease by the age of 35.

Within a few years of gaining control, Papa Doc made it plain he would share his power with no-one. Most of the finance from the United States was funnelled into his own private bank accounts while he lived in seclusion in his palatial presidential mansion. In 1961 he declared himself president for life and ordered the ill-disciplined Haitian Army to murder scores of political opponents. Their bodies were strung up on lamp posts around the capital, Port-au-Prince, with bloody voodoo symbols engraved on their corpses.

They had been killed, Papa Doc warned, by the forces of 'Baron Samedi', the avenging zombie of witchcraft. Baron Samedi, a hellish figure dressed in a black hat and a suit of mourning, was a voodoo demon, a soul raised from the dead to prowl the earth and carry out the wishes of the Devil.

To ensure that his own Army was in fear of him, Duvalier raised a secret police force, the Ton Ton Macoute – voodoo bogeymen who swore allegiance to him as the supreme witch doctor. The 10,000 members of the Ton Ton were given the task of killing hundreds of Army officers who were threatening rebellion against the bloodthirsty tyrant. In return they were given free rein to terrorise the countryside, looting and stealing from the starving peasants, carrying out murders which were always staged to bear the hallmarks of terrifying religious ritual.

The savagery of Papa Doc and his declaration of the grotesque cult of voodoo as Haiti's official national religion looked certain to prove his downfall. In the United States, recently elected President John F. Kennedy reacted with fury and indignation. Reflecting the civilised world's revulsion with Pap Doc's depravity, Kennedy announced that American aid to Haiti would cease as long as the Devil-worshipper was in power. It was thought to be only a matter of time before the pangs of hunger of the Haitians overcame their fear of demons and zombies. As the rumblings of discontent grew, even the gunmen of the Ton Ton Macoute were hard pressed to silence the increasing number of voices raised in anger against Duvalier.

For Papa Doc there was only one source of help to which he could turn. With power slowly beginning to slip from his grasp, he announced that he had performed a nightmarish voodoo ceremony to raise the Devil from Hell to put a curse on the American President. Six weeks later, John F. Kennedy died of an assassin's bullets in Dallas.

In Haiti the news was greeted with stunned despair. Nothing could shake the belief of terrified Haitians that the trigger of the assassin's gun had been pulled by the bony finger of the grinning zombie, Baron Samedi. Now Duvalier found new ways to bleed his people dry – literally. Still grasping for American dollars, he used the Ton Ton Macoute to round up thousands of Haitians daily and march them to medical centres in the capital, Port-au-Prince. There, each was given a week's wages of £1 in exchange for a litre of blood. The blood was flown to America and sold for transfusion at £12 a litre.

Papa Doc continued to rule supreme in Haiti. Any challenge to his power was met swiftly by the murder squads of the Ton Ton Macoute. In 1971, dying of diabetes and heart disease, he altered the constitution of Haiti to allow his podgy playboy son Jean-Claude, known as Baby Doc, to assume the mantle of power . . . Papa Doc had been president for life. Now he was trying to ensure that his devilish dynasty survived even in death.

Josef Stalin

Bolshevik bullets finally ended 400 years of repressive rule by Russia's Tsars. Nicholas II, gunned down with his haemophilic son Alexei in the cellar of a house in Ekaterinburg in July 1918, had fought to the last against what he called the 'senseless dream' of the people having a say in how their lives were governed. Bolstered in his belief in absolute autocracy by the sinister 'mad monk' Rasputin, he allowed ruthless henchmen to try to silence with savagery the growing clamour for basic human rights.

Chief of police Vyacheslav von Plehve mounted pogroms in Kishiniov and Gomel to 'drown the revolution in Jewish blood.' Minister of the Interior Peter Stolypin executed so many people for political offences – 5,000 in less than two years – that the gallows were nicknamed Stolypin's Necktie. And on Bloody Sunday, 22 January 1905, when riflemen and Cossack horsemen killed 150 defenceless men, women and children and injured a thousand more by brutally attacking a peaceful protest march to the St Petersburg Winter Palace, the Tsar's only question was: 'Have they killed enough?'

But there was by then no way that the revolution could be prevented. All it needed was a catalyst . . . and that came with the carnage of World War One, in which Russia lost vast tracts of land and 4 million men.

By 1916 abysmal leadership and terrible suffering had sapped the army's strength. And a year later, when soldiers and sailors garrisoned near St Petersburg sided with the strikers protesting at food shortages, inflation and corruption, the Tsar was forced to abdicate. The dreaded Ochrana, the secret police who maintained his reign of terror, were disbanded. Land confiscated from the rich was given to the peasants. Workers were promised an eight-hour day. Genuinely free elections were called. To the suddenly unsuppressed masses, Utopia seemed theirs.

But the revolutionaries had inherited a bitter legacy. In maintaining power at all costs, the Tsars had neglected the nation's interests. Revolutionaries like Lenin, returning from exile, knew from first-hand experience in Europe how backward the country was. 'Our task,' Lenin told his Politburo colleagues, 'is to take the lead of the exhausted masses who are wearily seeking a way out and lead them along the true path, along the path of labour discipline . . .'

But Lenin died in 1924, having taken only a few steps along that path. And his successor was to turn the democratic dream into a blood-soaked nightmare of tyranny on a scale that even the most sadistic Tsars never contemplated. In just

30 years of power, Josef Stalin killed more people than the Tsars had accounted for in four centuries. He turned a popular revolution based on ideals of freedom and equality into a totalitarian dictatorship maintained solely by terror. Although in the process he turned the Soviet Union into one of the world's two great super-powers, and extended its empire far beyond the boundaries established by the Tsars, even the communists who succeeded him denounced his monstrous excesses.

The dying Lenin had warned the communist Central Committee against Stalin, the shoemaker's son who had robbed banks in his native Georgia to raise funds for the Bolshevik cause, and rose to become party General Secretary in 1922. Lenin urged his colleagues to find someone 'more tolerant, more loyal, more polite, more considerate, less capricious,' and added: 'Comrade Stalin has concentrated boundless authority in his hands and I am not sure whether he will always be capable of using that authority with sufficient caution . . .' The party hierarchy did what they could, appointing Comrades Zinoviev and Kamenev to share leadership with Stalin. But already he was too powerful to be shackled. Adroit manoeuvring of the Politburo power blocs enabled him to demote, expel, even exile all potential rivals. By 1928 he was undisputed master of Moscow. Nikolai Bukhanin, one of Lenin's closest aides, confided to a friend when he was ousted: 'Stalin is a Genghis Khan who will kill us all.' It was a chillingly accurate prediction.

Stalin decided to accelerate Russian development. Huge new coal, iron and steel complexes were built all over Russia at a tremendous cost in human life. One of the American engineers called in as a consultant said: 'I would wager that Russia's battle of ferrous metallurgy alone involved more casualties than the Battle of the Marne.'

The programme was partly financed by swingeing taxes on richer peasants, the kulaks, who had been allowed by Lenin to sell surplus food to ease shortages. Dogmatic Stalin allowed no such 'deviations.' Soon the kulaks lost not only the

Walter Krivitsky was Stalin's military intelligence chief in Western Europe until he defected to escape a purge in 1936. He told a British interrogator: 'If you ever hear I have committed suicide, don't believe it. I will have been murdered.' In February 1941 his body was found in a hotel room in Washington DC. An inquest studied farewell notes before deciding that bullet wounds to his head were self-inflicted. But Krivitsky's widow Tania said of the notes: 'The writing is Walter's but the words are not.'

right to sell but their land and livestock. Stalin announced the elimination of the kulaks as a class. Millions were ordered to join vast state-run collective farms. Millions more were herded to towns to become forced labour in the new state-owned factories. Others disappeared into the growing network of 'corrective labour camps', the harsh 'Gulags' much later exposed by writer Alexander Solzhenitsyn. More than 25 million were forcibly evicted. More than three million were killed.

Stalin – the revolutionary name meant 'Man of Steel' – imposed his Marxist will on all walks of life. The party and government bureaucracies were purged of 'unreliable' workers – 164,000 Moscow civil servants were kicked out in 18 months. Church publications were suppressed, church buildings confiscated and the leaders exiled or jailed. Local nationalism in satellite states was dismissed as another 'deviation' and ruthlessly eradicated. Writers were subjected to intense censorship to ensure they wrote only work to inspire the proletariat. 'Where else do they kill people for writing poetry?' one artist asked plaintively. The grip of the secret police, the OGPU, tightened over everyone. Internal passports were re-introduced to make keeping track of people easier. Often alleged enemies of the state were quietly liquidated without troubling the courts. After all, the OGPU were working for a man who said: 'The death of a man is a tragedy; the death of a thousand is a statistic.'

Statistically the first five-year plan was a success. By 1935 industrial production was four times greater than in 1913. But progress had been bought at staggering cost. Results of a census in 1937 were so appalling they were suppressed. Two years later experts estimated that Russia's population was an astounding 20 million short of what it should have been. Emigration and famine

Stalin set up a special overseas sabotage and murder squad within his secret service in January 1946. Its first chief, war hero Pavl Anatolevich Sudoplatov, gave one officer – who later defected – this advice on recruiting killers: 'Go search for people who are hurt by fate or nature – the ugly, those suffering from an inferiority complex, craving power and influence but defeated by unfavourable circumstances. The sense of belonging to an influential, powerful organization will give them a feeling of superiority over the handsome and prosperous people around them and for the first time in their lives they will experience a sense of importance. It is sad and humanly shallow but we are obliged to profit from it.'

were factors. But Stalin's purges and the breakneck pace of industrialization accounted for many millions more. Historian E.H. Carr wrote: 'Seldom perhaps in history has so monstrous a price been paid for so monumental an achievement.'

In November 1932 Stalin's wife Nadezhda Alliluevna committed suicide with a revolver. At one time she had helped Stalin, telling him secrets learned from her job as a confidential code clerk in Lenin's private office. Now she was appalled at his increasingly brutal nature. He had become a foul-mouthed drunkard prone to violent rages, abusing underlings and indulging in debauched delights to test their loyalty. On one occasion he rolled five slim tubes of paper and stuck them on his secretary's fingers. Then he lit each like a candle and grinned as the man writhed in agony, not daring to remove them. Nadezhda's death removed one of the few remaining checks on Stalin's absolute authority. Their daughter Svêtlana said later: 'It deprived his soul of the last vestiges of human warmth.'

Then, in December 1934, a young communist shot dead party secretary Sergei Kirov in St Petersburg – which had been renamed Leningrad. Stalin instantly ordered the security services to speed up cases against people accused of executing or preparing to execute acts of terror. And he told courts to carry out death sentences immediately, since the government would no longer consider petitions for possible pardons. The ruling, as Nikita Khruschev later said, was 'the basis for mass acts of abuse against socialist legality.'

Stalin now began moving against old revolutionary colleagues. Zinoviev, Kamenev, Bukhanin and OGPU chief Yahoda were just four of the prominent communists accused of conspiring against the state in a series of show trials which lasted from 1936 to 1938. Astonishingly, they all pleaded guilty, perhaps through loyalty to the revolution, but more probably because they had been broken by torture and warned that their families would suffer if they caused a stir. By 1939, of the 139-strong Central Committee, 98 had been shot, and every member of Lenin's Politburo except Stalin himself and Trotsky, exiled in 1929, had been condemned by the courts.

New massive purges began throughout society. The Red Army leadership was more than halved. Naval top brass was devastated. The Communist Party rank and file was cleansed of intellectual idealists who put principles before the new politics of power, privilege and practicalities. Ruthless sycophants took their places, men with whom Stalin felt more secure. The secret police were shaken up and renamed the NKVD, under the notorious Beria. Even secret agents abroad, including spies who recruited and controlled English traitors Philby, Blunt and Burgess, were summoned back to Moscow and eliminated. Stalin, who knew more than most about conspiracy, saw plots everywhere. Others had to die because they knew too much about his previous misdeeds.

More than 500,000 people were summarily shot. Millions more were tortured and incarcerated. Even President Kalinin's wife spent seven years in a prison camp to guarantee her husband's behaviour.

The purges suddenly ceased in 1939. With the promise of a new, liberal constitution, people began to breathe more easily. But their relief was short-lived, for World War Two was about to begin . . .

To the war-weary nations allied against the Nazis, Soviet Marshal Stalin was avuncular Uncle Joe, a hero helping America and Britain end the evil of Hitler. Winston Churchill posed for photographs with him at the Yalta summit, and told journalists Stalin's life was 'precious to the hopes and hearts of us all.' He added: 'I walk through this world with greater courage when I find myself in a relation of friendship and intimacy with this great man.' It was not a sentiment shared by many of the millions who entered the war under Stalin, or the peoples he subjected during the hostilities. For Stalin's smiles at Yalta concealed a cruel and calculating nature prepared to condone and commit war crimes at least as evil as those of the enemy, and an ambition which was already bent on betraying the leaders who sang his praises.

Stalin had already betrayed the Allies once when, in August 1939, he had signed a non-aggression pact with Hitler. It was a cynical deal between a man who secretly planned to murder 30 million Slavs and a man who was already well on his way to doing so. Under its terms, the NKVD and the Gestapo compared notes on dissident refugees. Jewish prisoners in Soviet Gulags were swapped for concentration camp inmates Stalin wanted to get his hands on. Germany was allowed to use Murmansk as a submarine base and Russia supplied the Nazis with vital war materials. Most importantly for Stalin, he was given a free hand in certain areas to extend his reign of terror.

The Red Army marched into the Balkan states, ostensibly to preserve their neutrality. When Finland refused to hand over strategically useful land and islands, Stalin invaded to force the transfer at gunpoint. But it was Poland, a traditional enemy of Russia for centuries, which was most callously abused. The two dictators had drawn a line down the middle of the independent state. When Hitler invaded from the west, forcing Britain and France to declare war, Stalin's troops went in from the east, taking cruel advantage of Polish preoccupation with the Nazi attack. More than a quarter of a million Polish officers and men were captured – and 14,000 were never seen alive again.

In all the captured countries, the sinister NKVD arrived soon after the army had established control. They eliminated political and cultural leaders who might stand in the way of Stalin's planned Russification of the different nationalities. Millions were transported to the remote wastelands of Russia. Others were simply shot. As were Russians returned from captivity by the Finns. Stalin had no time for Soviet soldiers who failed him.

The fate of some of the missing Poles was revealed in 1943. The bodies of 4,000 officers were unearthed in shallow graves beneath a grove of young conifers at Katyn, near Smolensk. Most had their hands tied behind their backs and bullet wounds in the back of their necks. A few had smashed skulls. Some had straw or sawdust stuffed in their mouths, to kill them while saving ammunition. What happened to the remaining 10,000 who vanished has never been conclusively established, but some experts suspect they were loaded on barges and drowned in the White Sea by the NKVD. The missing included 800 doctors and 12 university professors.

Stalin was able to indulge himself in such blood-letting against his own and other peoples because he trusted Hitler. But by late 1940, the Führer was the master of mainland Europe, and able to prepare for the move he had planned all along: Operation Barbarossa, the invasion of Russia.

When Hitler's troops crossed the border at dawn on 22 June, 1941, Stalin was stunned. For 11 days he did nothing as the Red Army, weakened by purges and assured by their leader that invasion was impossible, fell back in disarray. But Stalin was eventually stung into action, when it became clear that many of his subjects were not resisting the Nazis, but welcoming them as liberators.

Long-silent church bells rang out in occupied towns as a religious people, denied the right to worship for years, joyously assembled for services. Civilians began hoping for the freedoms promised in 1917. Even the Jews, victims of Stalin's anti-semitism, responded willingly to Nazi posters asking them to register with the invaders. Nobody dreamed that Hitler could be as murderous a master as Stalin. Disillusioned Russian troops surrendered in droves. In less than six months, the invading army of just over 3 million captured nearly 4 million of the Red Army.

But Hitler and his army threw away their chances of capitalizing on Russian misery. Freed towns were soon appalled by the cruelty of the occupying forces. Hitler himself refused to allow nearly 800,000 Russian volunteers to fight for him

Stalin was a sadist. He liked to watch interrogations of political suspects by his secret police, and is quoted as ordering them to 'beat, beat and beat again until they come crawling to you on their bellies with confessions in their teeth.' Some historians attribute such brutality to the savage beatings he took from his father, a Georgian shoemaker who drank heavily. A childhood attack of smallpox, which left Stalin pockmarked for life, also contributed to his bitter inferiority complex.

against Stalin under rebel general Alexander Vlasov. And when Stalin appealed over the radio to 'his friends' the Russian people, they rose heroically to throw off the Nazi yoke.

Yet while his troops were battling back with courage, and Stalin was appealing to the Allies to send him battalions of reinforcements or to invade Europe to open a second front, the NKVD were waging war on the Russian people. Fearful of anyone who might try to topple him for his earlier savagery or for his military mistakes, Stalin launched yet another great purge. Army officers were killed by the hundred. Gulag inmates were slaughtered by the thousand. Potential 'enemies of the people' were massacred in every area that might fall into German hands. In his book *Stalin's Secret War*, Count Nikolai Tolstoy wrote: 'At Lvov, as the Soviet 4th Army battled against odds to save the city, the NKVD was working for a week with machine guns, grenades and high explosives in its frantic effort to liquidate thousands of Ukrainian prisoners. Thousands more were being transferred east under heavy armed guard.'

The Germans knew how Stalin dealt with Ukrainians. They had uncovered a mass grave of 9,000 bodies, clinically laid head to toe to save space, in the Ukrainian town of Vinnitsa, population 70,000. Again, most had their hands bound and bullet wounds in the back of the neck. Nazi propaganda chief Joseph Goebbels was making a rare excursion into truth when he said: 'If the Germans lay down their arms, the whole of eastern and south-eastern Europe, together with the Reich, would come under Russian occupation. Behind an iron screen, mass butcheries of people would begin, and all that would remain would be a crude automaton, a dull fermenting mass of millions of proletarians and despairing slave animals knowing nothing of the outside world.'

Slowly the Red Army pushed back the Germans and began pursuing them beyond Russia's borders. At their Yalta summit, the Allied leaders had agreed how to divide the spoils, once Hitler was forced into unconditional surrender. American forces held back to allow Stalin's troops to take Prague. In Poland, the Russians roused the Warsaw resistance via radio to attack their German oppressors and help the liberating army. Then the advance was halted for several days, giving Nazis time to kill as many Poles as possible.

By the end of the war, Stalin had added parts of Finland, Romania and Czechoslovakia, half of Poland and East Prussia, and most of the Baltic States to the Soviet Union. He had also established sympathetic buffer states in the rest of Czechoslovakia, Hungary, Bulgaria and Romania. And by entering the fighting against Japan after America dropped its A-bombs, he legitimized his annexation of the Kurile Islands, Sakhalin Island and parts of Mongolia. His sinister rule now stretched from the South China Sea to the River Elbe in Germany. And, just as Goebbels predicted, mass butchery began behind heavily policed borders.

Stalin in 1949

Beria's NKVD took savage revenge on anyone suspected of collaborating with the Nazis. Whole peoples from outlying areas – the Crimean Tatars, Kalmyks, Karachi-Balkars, Chechens – were transported to starvation in Siberia and Central Asia. Russian soldiers, returning either from captivity or victorious invasion, were thoroughly vetted. Those impressed by what they had seen in the West were shot or incarcerated. Stalin could not allow anyone to spread the word that the capitalist masses actually enjoyed a better standard of living than his Soviet proletariat. Even heroes suffered. Author Alexander Solzhenitsyn, twice decorated for bravery as an artillery officer, vanished into a Gulag for 8 years for 'insulting Stalin.' In the new satellite countries, loyal

Marxist-Leninists were executed or jailed after show trials and the communist parties purged of anyone not proved to be a committed Stalinist.

But the most terrible retribution leaked out only years later. At Yalta, Western leaders agreed to return to Stalin not just prisoners of war, but all refugees from his iron rule. The list ranged from Soviet citizens and soldiers who had tried to fight for Hitler to White Russians who had fled after the civil war ended in 1921. More than three million desperate escapees were in Western hands in 1945. By 1948 almost all had been forcibly repatriated. Britain alone sent 30,000. At Scarisbrook camp on Merseyside, one man hanged himself rather than fall into Stalin's clutches. Another cut his throat as he was led towards a ship on Liverpool dockside. In Rimini, Italy, British soldiers forced reluctant returnees to board trains at gunpoint. One man beat his brains out with a stone. Another was shot by troops as he tried to break free.

Back in the USSR, thousands of the helpless hostages were marched straight off boats and trains into makeshift execution yards. At ports on the north coast and in the Crimea, Soviet air force planes flew low to try to drown the sound of shooting. Those who escaped the quayside massacres were bundled into closed trains for a lingering death in the Gulags.

If Western governments hoped such sacrifices would satisfy Stalin, they were in for a shock. Instead of planning for peace, he ordered exhausted Russia into massive rearmament. Iron and steel production was trebled. Coal and oil targets were doubled. Hundreds of captured German scientists and technicians were forced to try to bridge the technology gap between the USSR and the West. The growing army of Moscow moles abroad was ordered to steal the secrets of the A-bomb. And the Soviet communist party was purged of anyone who refused to toe the hard-line Stalinist policy of cold war.

But the man hell-bent on imposing his brand of Soviet slavery on free nations was now a prisoner of his own terror. Otto Kuusinen, a Finn who knew Stalin better than most, said: 'The more ruthless and cold-blooded he became, the more he lived in an almost insane fear of his life.' Stalin's daughter Svetlana described her father as being 'as bitter as he could be against the whole world. He saw enemies everywhere. It had reached the point of being pathological, of persecution mania.'

Even in the Kremlin, Stalin wore a special bullet-proof vest. Tunnels were dug to link his office with other government buildings. Moscow's underground railway was secretly extended to his villa at Kuntsevo. When forced to appear above ground, Stalin used only an armour-plated car with bullet-proof windows 3 inches thick. NKVD squads checked out every route, and lined the roads when their leader drove past. All Stalin's food came from farms run by the NKVD. It was analyzed by a special team of doctors, served by bodyguards posing as waiters, and always tested for poison by companions before Stalin took a mouthful. His tea had to come from specially sealed packs which were used just once, the rest being thrown away. When the woman who always prepared his tea was spotted taking leaves from a pack with a broken seal, she was thrown into Lubianka prison.

But even a man as powerful as Stalin could not cheat death for ever. On 5 March, 1953, he collapsed with a cerebral haemorrhage, aged 73, apparently in a fury because some of the Politburo opposed his plans to transport thousands of Soviet Jews to wasteland near the Chinese border. According to Czech defector Karel Kaplan, he had even more sinister plans in mind. Kaplan, who fled to the West in 1976, reported that in 1951 Stalin told leaders of the East European satellite states to prepare for all-out war to occupy Western Europe 'in three or four years at the most.'

Stalin had taken Russia from the wooden plough to the nuclear age in 30 years. He had caught up with the advanced countries who had spent centuries making the transition. But in the process, the lives of more than 20 million Soviet citizens had been sacrified. Another 14 million were still in Gulag camps when he died. Count Nikolai Tolstoy wrote that, in a nation of 200 million people, 'scarcely a family had been untouched by tragedy.' It was too much even for the stomachs of those who succeeded Stalin as Soviet leaders.

The NKVD apparatus of fear, which had mushroomed to 1½ million men and women, was slimmed down and renamed the KGB. Beria and other powerful aides were shot within months of their patron's death. In 1956 Nikita Khruschev accused the man for whom he had once worked of unjustified harshness against 'punished peoples' and Russians captured by the Nazis. He also attacked Stalin for killing 'many thousands of honest and innocent communists.' And he added: 'Arbitrary behaviour by one person encouraged and permitted arbitrariness in others. Mass arrests and deportations of many thousands of people, execution without trial and without normal investigation created conditions of insecurity, fear and even desperation.'

Slowly Stalin slipped from public adulation in Russia as revelations about the means he used overshadowed the ends he achieved. In 1961 his remains were removed from the Red Square mausoleum and buried outside the Kremlin walls. His entry in Soviet encyclopaedias shrank. In 1977 his name vanished from the national anthem, though Lenin's stayed. But the most telling blow was a name change which symbolized the passing of two of the world's most repressive regimes. The Volga town of Tsaritsyn was retitled Stalingrad in honour of Stalin's gallant defence of it during the Russian civil war. Within a few years of his death, it became known as Volgograd.

Chapter Two

MERCILESS DESPOTS

The scourge of the sword . . . throughout history it has been the violent recourse of rulers who tortured and ravaged in their greed for conquest and power.

'Power takes as ingratitude the writhings of its victims.'

Rabindranath Tagore (1916)

Attila the Hun

Mass slaughter, rape and pillage were an integral part of life for most of northern Europe for centuries. Though the Greeks and Romans established the Mediterranean as the cradle of civilization, it was constantly rocked by murderous incursions from barbarian hordes to the north. Greek historian Herodotus, born in 484 BC, described savage Scythians north of the Black Sea who skinned opponents to make coats, sawed off the top of their skulls to make drinking cups and drank the blood of their victims. Wild Goths swept south from Sweden, and in AD 410 sacked Rome in a six-day orgy of rape and killing. Vicious Vandals reached the city less than 50 years later after storming through Germany, Gaul, Spain and North Africa, leaving death and destruction in their wake. Saxons, Franks and Vikings were other warlike and unmerciful raiders. But of all the brutal barbarians who terrorized Europe, none struck greater fear in men's hearts than a tribe whose roots were in the harsh steppes of Mongolia.

The Huns were wild horsemen driven out of their homeland by the Chinese in the second century AD. They rode west, conquering and cold-bloodedly massacring any tribe that stood in their way. Eventually they settled north of the river Danube, between the Volga and the Don, and established uneasy detente with neighbouring Romans, even helping the legions subdue troublesome tribes. Rome paid the Huns' King Ruas an annual tribute of 350 pounds of gold, but in return took hostages as a guarantee of good behaviour. The king's nephew, Attila, born in AD 406, spent part of his youth as a hostage in Italy. It was invaluable experience for a leader whose bloodthirsty campaigns were to earn him the title 'Scourge Of God'. Attila the Hun was 27 when King Ruas died. At first he ruled jointly with his brother Bleda, strengthening the kingdom by defeating Teutonic tribes like the Ostrogoths and Gepidae. By AD 444 he had complete control of the territory known today as Hungary and Romania. And he was absolute ruler after having his brother murdered. Now his ruthless ambition was ready to take on the Romans. The plaintive plea of a damsel in distress gave him the pretext for war.

Honoria, sister of Roman emperor Valentinian III, caused a scandal by having an affair with a court chamberlain and getting pregnant. Valentinian had her sent off to Constantinople, where she lived with religious relatives virtually a prisoner. Frustrated and bored, she smuggled her ring together with a message for help to Attila at his camp near Budapest, offering herself as his

Attila, King of the Huns

bride if he rescued her. The Hun chieftain already had as many wives as he needed, but he made the most of the request. He asked Valentinian for Honoria's hand – and half the Roman Empire as dowry. Rejected, he unleashed a furious onslaught.

His hordes swept south, through Macedonia – now mostly part of Greece – to the gates of Constantinople in AD 447. The Romans bought him off, increasing their yearly tribute to 2,100 pounds of gold, and paying a heavy indemnity for withdrawal. Attila went home with his booty, but four years later he led a vast army of Huns, Franks and Vandals across the Rhine into Gaul.

Town after town was ravaged and razed, but as the unscrupulous barbarians were about to storm the city of Orléans, the city was saved by the arrival of Roman legions allied to an army of Visigoths. Attila withdrew to the plains near Châlons-sur-Marne and prepared for battle. It lasted all day, with appalling carnage on both sides. One eye-witness later described the hand-to-hand fighting as 'ruthless, immense, obstinate.' The Visigoth king was just one of the thousands slaughtered. But Attila was forced to retreat back beyond the Rhine. Historians describe the battle as one of the most crucial ever. Had the Romans not won, they say, Europeans might today have slant-eyed, Mongol-like features.

Attila was bloodied but unbowed. A year later his men again swarmed south into Italy. Aquileia, the major city in the province of Venetia, was completely destroyed after appalling atrocities against its inhabitants. The Hun hordes swept on to the Adriatic sea, slaughtering the civilians of Concordia, Altinum and Padua before burning their properties. Frightened refugees fled to the islands and lagoons where horsemen could not follow. There they established the city we know as Venice.

The power-crazed heathen turned his army towards the Lombardy plain and Milan, plundering and pillaging until northern Italy was devastated. As Rome itself was threatened, Pope Leo I courageously left the Vatican for a personal interview with the irresistible invader. Attila, his fury subdued by such a bold move, agreed to lead his men home, though he talked menacingly of returning if Honoria's wrongs were not righted.

But there were to be no more atrocities from the most ruthless despot the world had then known. On 15 March, AD 453, he hosted a gigantic banquet to celebrate the taking of yet another wife, the beautiful virgin Ildico. That night, as he tried to consummate the marriage, an artery burst, and bloodthirsty Attila bled to death.

History has hailed Peter the Great as the Tsar who civilized Russia by introducing European customs and by fostering trade. In fact, he could be just as barbarous as Ivan the Terrible. When troops mutinied in Moscow in 1698, Peter personally supervised bloody reprisals which left 1,200 of them dead. For two months, men were flogged, broken on the rack or roasted slowly over flames. Peter was seen wielding an executioner's axe with relish. And he insisted that mutilated bodies be left on display for months as a warning to others.

Genghis Khan

Nearly 800 years after Attila's demise, Europe was reeling from the onslaught of another Mongol conqueror whose callous cunning and cruelty have never been matched. He was born in 1162 and named Temuchin after a tribal chief his father Yesukai had just defeated. At the age of 13 Yesukai's death in an ambush plunged the boy into the terror and treachery of tribal infighting. But he proved equal to every challenge. He cold-bloodedly killed one of his brothers in a dispute over a fish. He slaughtered every man, woman and child in a tribe of nomads who dared to kidnap his wife. And though rivals battled bitterly – one boiled 70 of his followers alive in cooking pots – by the spring of 1206 Temuchin was powerful enough to impose his power on all the Mongol tribes. He summoned leaders of dozens of warring factions to a conference on the banks of the river Onon and proclaimed himself their chief. He also took a new name – Genghis Khan, which meant perfect warrior.

China was first to feel his wrath. The Kin Tartars ruled the northern half of the country, and had been glad to accept when Genghis offered them some of his troops to suppress troublemakers. In 1211 that move rebounded on them. The troops had gained a comprehensive knowledge of the land inside the Great Wall, and even subverted sentries at some of the gates. The Mongol armies poured south, besieging and sacking cities, trampling and burning crops. By 1214 Genghis Khan controlled almost all the country north of the Yellow River. He offered the Kin emperor peace, adding: 'It will be necessary that you distribute largess to my officers and men to appease their fierce hostility.' Two royal princesses, 500 young men and girls, 3,000 horses and a herd of rare white camels were among the prizes the Mongol armies carried home. But within a year they were back, ruthlessly besieging the few cities that had survived the previous invasion.

Genghis Khan's empire was soon secure, ruled by a regime of fear which meant instant death to any rebel. The savage warlord now looked to the west and his neighbours the Khwarizms. Their vast territories stretched from the Ganges to the Tigris, and included present-day Turkistan, Iran and northern India. Genghis sent envoys to Shah Mohammed, promising peace and proposing trade. The reply seemed favourable. But when the first caravan of 100 Mongol traders arrived in the border town of Otrar, governor Inaljuk had them all massacred as spies. Furious Genghis sent more envoys, demanding the governor's extradition. Mohammed beheaded their leader and sent the rest home minus their beards. The insult was to cost the Shah his kingdom – and bring unprecedented horror to Europe's door.

More than 400,000 Khwarizm troops were strung along the Syr Daria river to repel the invasion, but they were like lambs to the slaughter when the Mongol armies struck in a three-pronged attack. One army attacked in the south, threatening the strategic cities of Bukhara and Samarkand. Two others crossed the mountains to the north and besieged Otrar. A bitter battle ended with the errant governor being executed as painfully as possible – molten metal was poured into his eyes and ears. Then, while one army turned south to link with the first near Bukhara, 40,000 men led by Genghis Khan vanished into the vast Kizylkum desert. They re-emerged behind Bukhara and behind the enemies' lines. The Shah fled as the city suffered the Mongol victory rites. Its mercenary defenders were slaughtered, and the civilians ordered outside what was left of the walls to allow uninterrupted looting. Then the women were raped in front of their families, craftsmen were taken as slaves and the remaining residents put to the sword.

The terror-struck Khwarizms had no answer to the Mongols' devastating military efficiency. Their infantry was helpless against hordes of horsemen who unleashed waves of arrows which decimated defenders, then moved in to finish them off ruthlessly with their curved sabres and lances. If a city or a pass seemed too secure, the Mongols would appear to retreat, then turn and scatter their pursuers with savage ferocity. As they moved further into Khwarizm territory, they herded crowds of captives in front of them as a human shield. Giant catapults, manned by up to 100 Mongol warriors, hurled rocks at city walls. Other defences were breached by means of a weapon unknown to the West, gunpowder.

Towns which opened their gates to the invaders were spared. Those that fought, like Samarkand, were not. The Mongols arrived in May 1220 to find a garrison of 50,000 men well dug in. When the attackers pretended to flee, the defenders poured after them and were cut to ribbons. When half the mercenaries deserted to Genghis Khan, the civilians surrendered, leaving soldiers besieged in the citadel. They were starved out and killed – then the turncoat mercenaries were massacred for treachery. Nearly 30,000 civilians were herded away to form a living shield at the next siege.

At Urgenj, the Mongols slaughtered every man and took the women and children as slaves before breaching dykes to flood the burning ruins. In Termez every body was cut open after Genghis discovered that one old woman had swallowed some pearls. At Nisa, Genghis's son Tulé had all the inhabitants' hands tied behind their backs, then watched them die in a hail of arrows. At Merv the poor were beheaded while the rich were savagely tortured to reveal the whereabouts of their treasures. When Nishapur surrendered, the severed heads of the residents were arranged in three gruesome pyramids of men, women and children.

Shah Mohammed had been broken by the speed and savagery with which his empire had been destroyed. He fled to a village on the Caspian Sea, and died of pleurisy. Genghis pursued his son and successor, Jelaleddin, south through Afghanistan, slaughtering hundreds of thousands of innocent civilians as he went. When his quarry took refuge with the Sultan of Delhi, the Mongols ravaged Lahore, Peshawar and Melikpur before turning north west again. News had reached Genghis that the people of Herat, spared after surrendering without a fight, had deposed the governor he installed. A six-month siege by 80,000 men ended the rebellion. Then a week of unbridled murder meted out the punishment. Thousands of corpses lay in the rubble of the city when Genghis at last headed for home. He had unfinished business with the Tangut tribe, who had declined to send troops to aid his Khwarizm campaign. He vowed to exterminate them all.

But age and weakness following a hunting accident were finally to achieve what no foe could manage. Genghis Khan was besieging the Tangut capital of Ninghsia in August 1227, when he fell ill and died, aged 65. His will named his son Ogotai as successor, but the warlord's aides decided that the death must remain secret until Ogotai was safely in command. The final victims of the man described by one historian as the 'mightiest and most bloodthirsty conqueror of all time' were the innocent souls who accidentally spotted the funeral procession as it headed for the burial ground in the valley of Kilien. Without exception, they were put to the sword.

Genghis Khan left an empire stretching from the China Sea to the Persian Gulf. But trembling neighbours who hoped his death would spare them further conquest were sadly mistaken. For the mighty Mongol had fathered a dynasty of ruthless rulers almost as callous and cruel. And they had their own territorial ambitions to extend their legacy.

Genghis's successor, Ogotai, spent his first years in power consolidating his grip on China and extending his empire in Korea. Then his avaricious eyes strayed westward again. The Mongol warriors surged through central Asia, laying waste to the cities of Tiflis and Ryazan, in Georgia, and massacring the

Not all deaths ordered by Genghis Khan were gory. Once he defeated another tribe led by a childhood friend. He offered to spare his life, but the rival insisted on execution. So Genghis decided to kill him without spilling blood. He was wrapped in a carpet and kicked to death.

inhabitants. Moscow, then an insignificant wooden township, was quickly taken. At Koselsk, revenge for an earlier reversal resulted in such a carnival of death that the laughing invaders renamed the town Mobalig, 'city of woe'. Finally Kiev, known as 'the mother of cities', was battered into submission. The residents were slaughtered and the buildings razed.

Now the Mongol army split. One of Genghis Khan's old lieutenants, Subatai, led a three-pronged assault on Hungary, aiming to rendezvous with the rest of the army at the Danube. But first the armies of Poland, Germany and Bohemia had to be prevented from coming to the aid of Hungary's fearsome Magyars. The rest of the invasion force swarmed into Poland, moving at a pace which staggered generals accustomed to slow-moving traditional battle strategy. The Poles were routed at Szydlow and the Germans at Liegnitz. The Bohemians beat a hasty retreat. In less than a month the Mongols had covered 400 miles, won two decisive battles, captured four major cities and cleared the way to the main objective – Hungary.

Hungarian King Bela IV had massed his men to meet Subatai at the Danube. But the Mongol commander declined to fight on ground which did not suit his horsemen. He began a calculated retreat to the Sajo river, and for six days the Hungarians followed, being lured further from their stronghold and reinforcements. Then Subatai turned for a savage dawn attack. Most of Bela's army was still asleep. By mid-day, more than 70,000 Magyars had been massacred. 'They fell to the left and right like leaves in winter,' wrote one chronicler. 'The roads for two days' journey from the field of battle were strewn with corpses as the rest tried to flee.'

Subatai stormed Budapest while part of his force chased King Bela to the Adriatic coast, burning and destroying everything in their path. On Christmas Day 1241 he led his forces across the iced-up Danube and took the city of Esztergom. But as Europe waited in trepidation for the next move, the Mongols again turned back. News had reached them that Ogotai was dead, and a bitter battle for succession was likely. No one wanted to miss it.

It was ten years before Genghis Khan's grandson Mangu, son of the tyrant Tulé, emerged as undisputed Mongol leader. Unrest in Persia, fostered by the Ismailites, prompted him to send his brother Halagu to the Middle East to storm the strongholds of a sinister sect known as the Assassins. Halagu rode on to Baghdad, then the major city in the region. After resisting for a month, the city

Genghis Khan gave the Mongols their first written laws, the Great Jasagh. Refusing to work, urinating in running water and gluttony all received the same sentence – death.

surrendered in February 1258. Halagu's marauders massacred everybody inside, trampling the sultan to death under horses. They set fire to the city, then turned towards Syria. Aleppo was sacked, Damascus surrendered, and Halagu was about to attack Jerusalem when, once again, a single death prevented thousands. The news was received that Mangu had died, and the hordes rode home.

Mangu's brother was Kubla Khan, celebrated in Coleridge's verse. Alone amongst the family, he treated captives humanely and banned indiscriminate massacres. For 34 years he concentrated on conquests in the East, in southern China, Tibet and Vietnam. He even tried to invade Japan without success. And after his death, the empire fell apart as his heirs squabbled. Even the Chinese cast off the Mongol yoke as the Ming Dynasty forced the wild warriors back to their Mongolian homeland.

Tamerlane the Great

The world had not heard the last of the merciless Mongols. In 1336 a boy called Timur was born at Kesh, near Samarkand. He was the great-great-grandson of Genghis Khan and conceived the desperate dream of rebuilding his forefather's empire, by then divided into a multitude of smaller principalities. Locals nicknamed him Timur i Leng, or Timur the Lame, because of a disability which made him limp. But the world remembers him as Tamerlane the Great, a wicked warmonger with a savage sadistic streak.

At 33 he usurped the Transoxian throne at Samarkand and gained the power base he needed for his conquests. Superb military management earned him mastery of Persia, Turkistan, the Ukraine, the Crimea, Georgia, Mesopotamia and Armenia. Governors who appealed to him for help frequently found themselves betrayed once he had restored their realms. He dethroned a rival khan to occupy Russia, then over-ran India, leaving a trail of carnage all the way to Delhi, where he reduced the city to rubble and massacred 100,000 inhabitants.

Like his ancestors, Tamerlane, tall with a huge head and white-haired from childhood, found that fear was no way to establish allegiance among the peoples he conquered. Revolts in the growing empire were frequent, but repressed ruthlessly. Whole cities were destroyed out of spite and their populations slaughtered. Massive towers or pyramids of skulls were constructed for the emperor's enjoyment. Twice he had thousands of opponents bricked up alive for agonising slow suffocation and starvation. Another time he hurled all his prisoners to their deaths over a cliff.

After his Indian campaign, Tamerlane stormed into Syria to settle old scores with leaders who refused to help in his earlier wars. Aleppo was seized and sacked and Damascus occupied in 1400. Baghdad, still smarting from Halagu's atrocities a century earlier, was devastated again by fire, and 20,000 people put to the sword. In 1402 Tamerlane unleashed his wrath on Anatolia – now Turkey – and beheaded 5,000 Ottoman fighters after one siege. Their sultan was killed in captivity in a barbarous iron cage.

The nightmare return to the depravity of an earlier age ended only with Tamerlane's death. His hordes were on their way to attack China when, in January, 1405, he fell ill while camping on the Syr Daria river and died. By a bizarre twist of fate, it happened at Otrar – the town whose governor had unwittingly sparked off the fury of the Mongols under Genghis Khan nearly 200 years earlier when he executed 100 traders. Millions had since paid the Mongols' bloody price for that rash act.

Ivan the Terrible

In July 1662, a mob of 5,000 angry Russians marched to the palace of Tsar Alexis in the suburbs of Moscow. Poor harvests and a long war with Poland had exhausted their patience over harsh taxation, currency devaluation and corrupt officialdom, and they extracted a promise from the Tsar that he would act on their grievances. But his solution to the problems was not what they had in mind. According to historian V.O. Klyuchevsky, 'Tsar Alexis called on the streltsy (musketeers who formed the Tsar's bodyguard) and his courtiers for assistance, and an indiscriminate slaughter ensued, followed by tortures and executions. Hundreds were drowned in the River Moskva and whole families were exiled permanently to Siberia.'

Alexis was pious and artistically-minded. He tried to leave government to ministers. But he had been born into a succession of Tsars who inherited absolute rule from the Mongols – and were equally merciless about maintaining it. Any challenge to their authority was met by torture, exile and execution. The loyalty of a few select aristocrats was bought with land and honours. The peasants – 90 per cent of the population – were shackled in medieval-style serfdom; denied education, the right to change jobs, even the right to choose their own marital partners. And if they grew restless about their lot, soldiers and a secret army of informers soon brought them back into line with bloodshed. For four centuries, the Tsars ruled Russia by fear. And few rulers inspired more fear than Ivan the Terrible.

Ivan, born in August 1530, was an orphan by the age of eight. His father Vasily, Grand Duke of Moscow, died when he was three. Five years later his mother Elena, who acted as Regent, was poisoned. After that, Ivan was to claim that he received 'no human care from any quarter.' Vicious power battles between leading families marked his early years. Ivan was used as a pawn by rival factions wrestling for control, only to lose it, in a succession of bloodbaths. He watched one of his uncles carried off to death by a Moscow mob in one uprising. But he quickly learned how to fight back. He was just 13 when he ordered his first assassination. Then he threw the body of his victim, a troublesome Shuisky prince, to his dogs.

In 1547, Ivan had himself crowned Tsar and, at a parade of the nation's most beautiful and eligible virgins, he selected himself a bride – 15-year-old Anastasia. She produced six children for him, but only two were still alive when she died in 1560. Their deaths, plus the loss of his wife's calming influence and the trauma of his childhood, may all have played a part in the horrors that followed.

First Ivan banished his closest advisers, his personal priest Father Silvestr, and nobleman Alexei Adashev, accusing them of plotting to kill Anastasia. Then he left Moscow for virtual monastic seclusion in the provinces. All sections of the community begged him to return, fearing a power vacuum. Ivan agreed – but only if he was allowed to govern without any interference. When his terms were accepted, he split the nation into two vast sections. In one, he was absolute master. The rest of the country was to be governed for him by bureaucrats.

Now Ivan unleashed unprecedented terror on his people, using the sinister oprichniki. They were black-cloaked riders on black horses, whose saddles carried the symbols of a broom and a dog's head. With unbridled fury, they slaughtered anyone suspected of opposition to Ivan, and settled many of his old scores from the turmoil of his teenage days. More than 4,000 aristocrats were purged. The Staritsky family, relatives of Ivan but potential rivals for power, were wiped out. When Metropolitan Philip, leader of the Orthodox Church in Moscow, condemned the oprichnikis' attacks and refused to bless the Tsar, the ruthless riders tracked him down and savagely executed him.

Ivan himself often took part in their orgies of rape, torture and death. And his rage really ran wild when an informant told him civic leaders of Novgorod, then Russia's second city, were planning rebellion. Without bothering to check the allegation, which was almost certainly untrue, Ivan led his oprichniki north, pillaging and plundering aristocratic homes, monasteries and churches within 50 miles of the city. Having laid waste to the fields that fed Novgorod, he then built a wooden wall around the metropolis to prevent anyone fleeing. And for five weeks, he watched, or took part in, wholesale slaughter.

Husbands and wives were forced to watch as their partners – and sometimes their children – were tortured. Many women were roasted alive on revolving spears. Other killings were treated almost as sport. One German mercenary wrote: 'Mounting a horse and brandishing a spear, he (Ivan) charged in and ran people through while his son watched the entertainment . . .'

Though Soviet scholars have claimed recently that no more than 2,000 people died, Western historians put the total toll in the annihilation of Novgorod at over 60,000. And Ivan's sadistic savagery there, and at Pskov, also suspected of plotting, certainly had an effect on later opponents. When he invaded neighbouring Livonia, one beseiged garrison blew themselves up rather than fall into his cruel clutches.

In 1572 Ivan suddenly disbanded the oprichniki and banned all mention of them. Throughout his life, his sadism alternated with periods of manic religious depression, when he would publicly confess his sins and don sackcloth. So perhaps genuine shame ended the six-year reign of terror. Perhaps an attack on Russia from the south by Turks forced him to call off internal vendettas. Or perhaps his assassins had eliminated almost everyone Ivan wanted out of the way.

Ivan got away with his ruthless rule because he had the support of the Orthodox Church. Western Europe was undergoing the religious crisis of the Reformation, and Orthodox leaders were terrified of free-thinking Protestantism which would weaken their hold on the unthinking masses. In exchange for a hard line on all religious dissent, including burning for 'heresy', the Church backed the Tsar and became an effective propaganda machine on his behalf. When peasant revolts were crushed with total brutality, the causes and the consequences were never attributed to Ivan. They were blamed on the corruption or excessive zeal of those who worked for him.

For a few Russians, Ivan was not so terrible. They were the people granted lands and power in the territories the Tsar added to his empire, north of the Black Sea and in Siberia. But the wars that won them, and campaigns which won nothing, forced an ever-increasing tax burden on Russian landowners and their peasants. And by the end of Ivan's reign, English ambassador Giles Fletcher was reporting to London: 'The desperate state of things at home maketh the people for the most part to wish for some foreign invasion, which they suppose to be the only means to rid them of the heavy yoke of his tyrannous government.'

In fact there was another way – Ivan's death. It came in March 1584, three years after he killed his son and heir Ivan with a spear during a quarrel. A life of licentiousness – six more wives and innumerable mistresses – had left the Tsar riddled with disease. As British trader Sir Jerome Horsey put it: 'The emperor began grievously to swell in his cods, with which he had most horribly offended above 50 years, boasting of a thousand virgins he had deflowered and thousands of children of his begetting destroyed.' Ivan collapsed and died as he prepared to play a game of chess.

Yet even his departure did not spare Russia agony. His heir's death left Ivan's imbecilic son Theodore as successor and he soon proved hopelessly unable to govern. The country was plunged into 30 years of chaos, which included occupation by the armies of both Poland and Sweden, before the Romanovs – relatives of Ivan's wife Anastasia – were able to reimpose the authority of the Tsars.

Historians still dispute whether Tsarist Russia's most bloodthirsty tyrant was consciously bad or completely mad. Some seek excuses in his traumatic childhood. Others blame a painful spinal defect for his excesses. It was nearly 350 years before Ivan the Terrible found sympathetic consideration from someone who believed his oprichniki had played a 'progressive role', someone who claimed his only mistake was not taking his purges further. That sympathiser was Josef Stalin. And as the earlier chapter on Stalin shows, he did not make the same 'mistake'.

The Ottoman Sultans

Turkey was known as the sick man of Europe throughout the 19th Century. Crisis followed crisis – one culminated in the bloody Crimea War – as the continent's super-powers bolstered the weak and crumbling regime of the once-great Ottoman Sultans to prevent rivals like Russia from seizing Constantinople and threatening trade routes. Then the outraged western world learned that Turkey was even sicker than they feared – but in a very different sense.

Like the Mongols before them, early Ottoman armies conquered mercilessly. Massacres of captives were commonplace, an accepted aspect of warfare. And by 1588 – the year Spain's Armada was routed by England – the Sultans ruled an empire which circled most of the Mediterranean. It stretched from the Red

Mahomet III

Sea port of Aden to Budapest and Belgrade, from the Crimea north of the Black Sea to Algeria. Huge chunks of present-day Hungary, Poland and Russia shared the same masters as the people of Greece, Egypt, Tunisia, Libya, Lebanon, Syria, Israel, Yugoslavia, Romania and Bulgaria. Any revolts among the 30 million subjects were ruthlessly suppressed.

But the absolute power of the Sultans not only corrupted them, it blinded them to the changing world outside their realms. In 1876 a rebellion in Bulgaria was repressed with traditional carnage. Ottoman troops ran amok in an orgy of killing, and more than 12,000 men, women and children were slaughtered. But by then the western world had newspapers, and millions were appalled to realise that medieval-style tyranny still went on in the 'modern' age. Historians were to discover that such tyranny had run virtually unchecked for 350 years – and would carry on well into the 20th Century.

The sinister Sultans had more reason than most absolute rulers to be paranoid about plots. A strong tradition of strangulation by deaf mutes, using silk bowstrings, existed inside the walls of their Grand Seraglio palace. Mahomet the Conqueror (1431–81) formulated a law by which his successors as Sultan had 'the right to execute their brothers to ensure the peace of the world.' It was designed to stop disputes over succession. But when Mahomet III took the throne in 1595, his father Murad III's prowess in the harem meant he had to murder 19 brothers, all aged under 11, and throw seven pregnant concubines into the Bosporus tied up in sacks.

Thereafter, close male relatives of the incoming Sultan were locked up in a windowless building within the Grand Seraglio complex until the Sultan's death called them to the throne. Cut off from the outside world, with only deaf mutes and sterilized concubines for company, many were completely deranged when they came to power, sometimes after more than 30 years incarceration. It was 1789 before the practice was abolished – and by then, madness was in the blood of the Ottoman dictators.

Suleiman the Magnificent, who ruled from 1520 to 1566, is regarded by most historians as the last great Sultan. In 1526 he seized more of Hungary, massacring 200,000 – 2,000 were killed for his enjoyment as he watched from a throne – and taking 100,000 slaves back to Constantinople. Three years later, when Vienna stubbornly refused to surrender, he scoured the surrounding countryside and selected the most nubile girls for Turkey's harems. Then he threw hundreds of unwanted peasants on a gigantic fire in view of the city walls. Such 'sanity' in the name of military strength was succeeded by a dynasty of Sultans who were weak, debauched, indecisive or insane – or sometimes all four.

Suleiman's son Selim II was a drunkard, despite the proscription of alcohol by the Koran, and decided to wrest Cyprus, source of his favourite wine, from its Venetian rulers. His soldiers sacked Nicosia, slaughtering 30,000. When the key fortress of Famagusta fell after a two-year siege, the Turks promised to spare the heroic garrison – then killed them all. Their commander was flayed alive, then paraded in front of the Turkish troops, his body stuffed with straw. Venice, Spain and Austria retaliated with the humiliating naval triumph of Lepanto, at which 50,000 Turks died. But the Ottomans still held Cyprus when, in 1574, Selim lost his footing climbing into his bath after a drinking session, and died from a fractured skull.

His son, Mahomet III, the man who killed his 19 young brothers, was a man with a fiery temper who enjoyed the sight of women's breasts being scorched off with hot irons. Osman II, who ruled for less than a year before his 1618 murder, enjoyed archery – but only if his targets were live prisoners-of-war or page boys. And while these two, and a string of insignificant Sultans, indulged themselves, the empire began to fall to pieces. Neglect and oppression ravaged the countryside, with tax income tumbling as famine laid waste to whole areas. The rigid disciplines which had made the Ottoman empire strong were also disintegrating.

Murad IV, a savage, dark-eyed giant, tried to reimpose them when he took over in 1623. After the Janissaries, the Sultan's special army, forced him to sack the chief minister and 16 other officials, he later revenged himself for their impudence by having more than 500 of their leaders strangled in their barracks. Then he set about the rest of the nation, as author Noel Barber records in his excellent book, *Lords Of The Golden Horn*.

'Murad quickly found a simple panacea for the ills of the country,' writes Barber. 'He cut off the head of any man who came under the slightest suspicion. In 1637 he executed 25,000 subjects in the name of justice, many by his own hand. He executed the Grand Mufti because he was dissatisfied with the state of the roads. He beheaded his chief musician for playing a Persian air. He liked to patrol the taverns at night and if he caught anyone smoking he declared himself and executed the offender on the spot. When he caught one of his gardeners and his wife smoking, he had their legs amputated and exhibited them in public while they bled to death.'

A Venetian who added a room to the top of his house was hanged because Murad thought he had done it to spy on the Sultan's harem. A Frenchman who arranged a date with a Turkish girl was impaled. And, according to Barber, Murad 'spent hours . . . exercising the royal prerogative of taking ten innocent lives a day as he practised his powers with the arquebus on passers-by who were too near the palace walls. On one occasion he drowned a party of women when he chanced to come across them in a meadow and took exception to the noise they were making. He ordered the batteries to open fire and sink a boatload of women on the Bosporous when their craft came too near the Seraglio walls . . .'

Murad's atrocities were not confined to home. In 1638 he led his troops to the Persian capital, Baghdad. After a six-week siege, during which he sliced in half the head of a Persian champion in single-handed combat, he ordered the massacre of the defending garrison of 30,000. When an accidental ammunition explosion killed some Turkish troops, Murad slaughtered 30,000 men, women and children.

But Murad was the last of the all-conquering Ottoman despots. His son Ibrahim's most notable conquest was deflowering the virgin daughter of the Grand Mufti, Turkey's highest religious leader. Then, when one concubine from his harem was seduced by an outsider, he had all 280 girls tied in weighted sacks and thrown into the Bosporus. Even Constantinople, which could forgive its Sultans almost anything, could not condone that. The Grand Mufti took revenge by organising a coup which toppled Ibrahim, then had him, his mother and his favourite lover strangled.

The Ottoman armies had long lost their invincible reputation. In 1683 an alliance of European forces crushed another attempt to take Vienna. In 1790 the Russian forces of Catherine the Great took Ismail, 40 miles north of the Black Sea, and dropped the corpses of 34,000 fallen Turks into the Danube through holes in the ice. In 1827, a six-year war, with massacres on both sides, ended with the Greeks winning independence. Egypt achieved a large measure of self-government.

The Ottoman empire was in steady decline. Elsewhere in the world, such events as the French Revolution, the American Constitution, with its declaration of rights, the Industrial Revolution, a more general right to vote and the introduction of newspapers had all helped foster an awareness of human rights which forced governments to act more humanely. But in 1876, the Ottoman Sultan showed just how far behind the tide of civilization his country had fallen.

In that year, the Bulgarians, who had been part of the Ottoman empire for nearly 500 years, revolted – and Sultan Abdul Aziz unleashed the bloodlust of unpaid troops who were rewarded only by what they could loot. Within days 12,000 men, women and children were dead and 60 villages burned to the ground. The Sultan gave the commander of the troops a medal.

The carnage in the town of Batak was witnessed by American journalist J. A. MacGahan and, when his report appeared in the *Daily News*, the stunned world had its first eye-witness account of an Ottoman atrocity. 'On every side as we entered the town were the skulls and skeletons of women and children,' he wrote. 'We entered the churchyard. The sight was more dreadful. The whole churchyard for three feet deep was festering with dead bodies partly covered. Hands, legs, arms and heads projected in ghastly confusion . . . I never imagined anything so fearful. There were three thousand bodies in the churchyard and the church. In the school 200 women and children had been burnt alive . . . no crime invented by Turkish ferocity was left uncommitted.'

Western governments at first refused to accept the reports, labelling them 'picturesque journalism.' But when Britain sent an investigator from the Constantinople embassy, he told Whitehall the troops had perpetrated 'perhaps the most heinous crime that has stained the history of the present century.' Ex-Prime Minister William Gladstone issued a pamphlet describing the Turks as 'the great anti-human specimen of humanity.' The storm of worldwide protest caused a coup which installed Abdul Aziz's drunken nephew Murad as Sultan. His reign lasted three months, until he was declared insane, and his brother Abdul Hamid II took over.

Abdul was so paranoid about possible plots that he built an entire village, designed only for his safety. Behind the barricades he kept loaded pistols in every room – two hung beside his bath – and constructed glass cupboards which, when opened, blasted the room with bullets from remote-controlled guns. He personally shot dead a gardener and a slave girl whose sudden movements alarmed him. He countered the growing revolt of the Young Turks with a network of spies and a torture chamber under a cruel executioner who delighted in slowly drowning broken men.

But his most astonishing act was to order the monstrous slaughter of the Armenians, a minority race whose homeland was in the north-east of the dwindling empire, close to the Russian border. He regarded the business-minded Armenians much as Hitler later regarded the Jews. First he banned the word 'Armenian' from newspapers and school books. Then he told Moslems they could seize Armenian goods – and kill the owners if they resisted.

Clearly, Abdul had learned nothing from the 1876 atrocities. And his massacres were far worse. It was cold-blooded, premeditated genocide. For days a bugle at dawn and dusk called the faithful to murder. Nearly 100,000 Armenians were killed. And Westerners witnessed the terror in Trebizond, where every Christian house was plundered before the owners were ritually slaughtered, their throats cut as if they were sheep. Those who jumped into the river to flee were caught and drowned by Moslem boatmen. At Urfa 3,000 men, women and children were roasted alive in the cathedral after seeking sanctuary. Sultan Abdul noted every detail as his spies sent detailed reports.

If the Sultan hoped to curry favour with his people, using racial prejudice to blind them to the economic ruin of his empire, he was sadly mistaken. Many Moslems felt only shame, labelling him Abdul the Damned. And this time, it was not only Europe that was outraged. Two Armenian professors at an American missionary school were arrested, taken in chains for trial for printing seditious leaflets, and sentenced to die. America was scandalized. Finally, when 7,000 Armenians were slaughtered in Constantinople in reprisal for a band raid carried out by 20, every European power signed an open telegram to the Sultan. If the massacres did not end at once, it read, the Sultan's throne and his dynasty would be imperilled.

Sultan Abdul Hamid survived to celebrate his Silver Jubilee as the new century dawned. But he was now an obsolete leftover from another age. And in 1908, the Young Turks – whose numbers and influence had been growing, first in exile, then in Turkey – seized power. The Sultan was exiled to Salonika and his brother, a stooge figurehead, installed as constitutional monarch. Sacks of gold and precious gems, a fortune in foreign bank accounts and shares in international companies were discovered at Abdul's palace, all obtained with money milked from the Turkish treasury.

The repressive rule of the Ottomans had finally ended. But if Turks and the West thought they had seen the end of evil and tyranny, they were in for a shock. For in 1915, Enver Bey, one of the three Young Turk leaders, ordered a new massacre of Armenians, even more ruthless than that of the Sultan. Using the

Abdul Hamid II, overthrown by the Young Turks in 1908

excuse that some Armenians had collaborated with the Russians during World War I battles – Turkey fought on the Kaiser's side – he made his brother-in-law Djevet Bey governor of the region, with orders to exterminate the Christians.

The inhabitants of more than 80 villages were rounded up and shot. Thousands of women were raped. Men were tortured, often by having horseshoes nailed to their feet. One official admitted he 'delved into the records of the Spanish Inquisition and adopted all the suggestions found there.' More than 18,000 Armenians were sent on a forced march of exile across the Syrian desert to Aleppo. Then Kurdish rebels were encouraged to attack them. Only 150 women and children reached Aleppo, 70 days after setting out.

The official British report on the atrocities, presented to Parliament, estimated that, of two million Armenians in Turkey in 1915, a third died and another third fled to Russia. The American Ambassador in Constantinople asked Enver Bey to condemn his underlings for the outrages. To his astonishment, the callous leader accepted responsibility for everything that had taken place. His co-leader, Talaat Bey, said it was unwise to punish only those Armenians who had actually helped the Russians 'since those who are innocent today might be guilty tomorrow.' And he had the audacity to ask the American Ambassador for a full list of Armenians covered by U.S. insurance companies. As their relatives were probably dead, he said, life assurance payments should go to the government.

Enver, Talaat and Djevet fled in November 1918, denounced for choosing the wrong side in a war which cost Turkey half a million battle casualties and for profiteering in food at a time of famine. The victorious allies took control in Constantinople. The empire was now smashed, and Turkey pushed back almost to its present borders. But to head off feared Italian territorial ambitions, the allies allowed the Greeks to occupy the port of Smyrna. Revenge for centuries of repression resulted in massacres of Turks – and fuelled the fury that, in atoning for wrongdoing, would make Turkey once again an international outcast.

Patriot Mustafa Kemal was the focus for Turkish anger at the allied occupation, and the loss of Smyrna. Though he was courtmartialled and sentenced to death in his absence, his support grew, and the allies were unable to control his rebel forces. Finally the Greeks offered their army to restore order. In 1920 their campaign pressed the Turks back. But in August 1921, Mustafa's men won a three-week battle along a 60-mile front at Sakkaria river. The Greeks fled towards the coast. The following year, reinforced by arms from France, Italy and Russia, the Turks again routed their most bitter foes, forcing them back to Smyrna. In September, Mustafa arrived in triumph at the port, and decreed that any Turkish soldier who molested civilians would be killed.

Peter the Great set up the first efficient secret police force in Russia and ruled by fear through a network of spies. He financed his almost constant wars by seizing Church assets and introducing bizarre taxes on beards, bee-keeping, coffins, clothes and foodstuffs. By the end of his reign, the peasants who made up 90 per cent of Russia's population were far worse off than when he came to power.

But within hours, the Greek Patriarch had been torn to pieces by a Turkish mob, under the eyes of the town's new commander. Mass looting, raping and killing began, Turkish troops methodically moving from house to house in the Greek and Armenian areas in the north of the town. 'By evening dead bodies were lying all over the streets,' said one American witness. Worse was to come. On Wednesday 13 September, Westerners saw squads of Turkish soldiers setting fire to houses in the Armenian quarter using petroleum. The wind spread the flames northwards, and thousands of flimsy homes were engulfed. Five hundred people perished in a church set ablaze deliberately. The reek of burning flesh filled the air. Tens of thousands fled to the waterfront, pursued by a rapidly growing wall of fire. In the bay lay warships from Britain, America, Italy and France. They were there to protect their nationals – but they had strict orders to maintain neutrality in the war between Greek and Turk. The sailors watched in horror as the inferno changed the colour of the sea and silhouetted the throng of helpless refugees on the wharfs. Then, at midnight, they heard what one described as 'the most awful scream one could ever imagine.'

Humanity over-rode orders next morning, when a massive rescue attempt began. Mustafa Kemal had said as he watched the fire: 'It is a sign that Turkey is purged of the traitors, the Christians, and of the foreigners, and that Turkey is for the Turks.' Three days after the blaze began, he announced that all Greek and Armenian men aged between 15 and 50 were to be deported inland in labour gangs. Women and children had to be out of Smyrna by 30 September or they too would be rounded up. He was later persuaded to extend the deadline by six days. Military and merchant ships performed a miracle, ferrying nearly 250,000 people to safety. No-one has ever been able to say how many corpses were left behind, though most estimates start at 100,000.

Mustafa Kemal always maintained that the Greeks and Armenians started the great fire of Smyrna. But a report for the American State Department said all the evidence pointed to an attempt by the Turks to hide evidence of 'sack, massacre and raping that had been going on for four days.'

Mustafa, oddly, later changed his name to Kamal Atatürk and instigated massive reforms throughout the government and society which finally dragged Turkey into the 20th Century. The last vestiges of the scourge of the Ottomans were buried forever.

Chapter Three

FOR GOD, KING AND COUNTRY

Twisted minds . . . of evil men who used the mask of religion or patriotism as an excuse for some of the most horrifying crimes in history.

'The belief in a supernatural source of evil is not necessary. Men alone are capable of every wickedness.'

Joseph Conrad (1911)

The Borgias

It was a city where the brazenly licentious indulged in perverse orgies and incestuous relationships. Where ambitious and greedy men grabbed power and personal fortune by bribery and extortion. And where anyone who stood in their way was ruthlessly eliminated. Yet the city where all this happened was not the hub of a barbarian empire. This citadel of sin was the Vatican City in Rome. And the evil masterminds putting vice before virtue, riches before religion and power before piety were the Pope, Alexander VI, alias Rodrigo Borgia, and his illegitimate son Cesare.

For centuries, the Catholic Church was the only Christian faith in Europe. But its monopoly on salvation brought corruption. It sanctioned merciless killing in crusades against so-called heathen-races who worshipped other gods. It exterminated as heretics all who dared question its edicts about the world and life. And it amassed immense wealth by charging a high price for forgiveness of sins. By the 15th Century, the Pope was not only a religious leader, but a powerful political force. Secular rulers in the confusing cluster of small states that made up the Italian peninsula competed for his favours and support – and his requests, backed by the threat of excommunication if they were refused, were compelling even for the strongest kings and princes.

Rodrigo Borgia was well grounded in the intrigues and intricacies of the Holy See long before he assumed its highest office. In April 1455, his mother's brother became Pope Calixtus III. Rodrigo, born 24 years earlier at Xativa, near Valencia in Spain, was immediately made a bishop, and quickly progressed up the Catholic hierarchy, to cardinal and vice-chancellor. He served in the Curia under five Popes.

But behind the facade of faith, hope and chastity, Rodrigo was busy seducing as many young virgins as he could lay his hands on. A highly sexed, handsome charmer, he could not resist the temptations of the flesh and one of his brazen open-air orgies earned him a reprimand from the Pope. In 1470 he began a torrid romance with a 28-year-old beauty, Vanozza dei Catanei. She bore him three sons, Giovanni (1474), Cesare (1476) and Goffredo (1481) and a daughter, Lucrezia (1480) before he tired of her and fell for the charms of the 16-year-old Giulia Farnese. For appearance's sake, he had Giulia betrothed to his young nephew – but he forbade the boy to consummate the marriage.

When Pope Innocent VIII died in 1492, Rodrigo was one of three contenders to become Pontiff. On the first poll, the electoral college of cardinals voted for

Cesare Borgia, Renaissance tyrant

Giuliano della Rovere, the successor nominated by Innocent. But Borgia began handing out huge bribes and promised delegates luxurious palaces and lucrative posts if he was chosen. On 10 August he duly became Pope, taking the name Alexander VI.

Instantly he showered his illegitimate children with riches. Cesare, aged just 16, was appointed Archbishop of Valencia. A year later he became a cardinal. But the titles meant little to the ambitious teenager. He was furious that his older brother had been given command of the Papal army. Cesare rode disdainfully round Rome, fully armed, with a succession of shapely mistresses at his side. He canoodled outrageously in public with his sister Lucrezia. And he rivalled his father's scandalous sexual exploits. When Sanchia, promiscuous teenage daughter of the King of Naples, arrived at the Vatican as a prospective bride for Goffredo Borgia, both the Pope and Cesare made a rigorous check on her credentials between the sheets of their own beds.

One of Cesare Borgia's few admirers was a man whose name later became synonymous with evil cunning: Niccolo Machiavelli. When the Papal army threatened Florence, Machiavelli, a city official, was sent to gauge Cesare's intentions. Borgia demanded gold in return for not attacking Florence. Machiavelli stalled while accompanying the army on conquests of other cities. He studied Cesare's ruthless methods, and used them as the basis for his book *The Prince.*

Its cynical dictates made survival of the state an end which justified any means. 'A prudent ruler ought not to keep faith when doing so would be against his interests,' Machiavelli wrote. Using force was justified if the rule of law proved insufficient, and governors were urged to give 'no consideration to either justice or injustice, to kindness or cruelty or to actions being praiseworthy or ignominious.' But Machiavelli was not an innovator advocating calculated corruption. He was a patriot who despaired because the squabbling states of Italy were too fragmented to stop France and Spain dominating the Italian peninsula. In Cesare Borgia he saw a man strong and unscrupulous enough to forge those states into a united nation. When Cesare lost power, Machiavelli passed on his hard-hearted philosophy in the hope that a later warrior would achieve the dream. And as a contemporary noted, Machiavelli's work contained little that was new. Though pious people thought him heretical and good people branded him wicked, the chronicler wrote: 'To the evil ones, he was merely too knowledgable in their ways.'

Rodrigo's reign began in embarrassing fashion. When King Ferrante of Naples died, the new Pope recognized the king's son Alphonso, father of saucy Sanchia, as successor. But the French King, Charles VIII, thought he had a better claim – and invaded Rome to prove it. Rodrigo grovelled and agreed to let Charles take Cesare along as a hostage on his journey south to the Naples coronation. But Cesare slipped away during the trip, returned to Rome and helped his father form an anti-French alliance with the rulers of Spain, Milan and Venice. Charles, afraid of being cut off from his homeland, scurried back to France and Alphonso was reinstated.

The Borgias then set about punishing those who had helped Charles to humiliate them. Cesare seized some Swiss mercenaries who had broken into his mother's home during the French occupation of Rome, and tortured them unmercifully. Rodrigo ordered the people of Florence to arrest and torture Girolamo Savonarola, a puritan monk who had denounced corruption in the Church and had welcomed Charles as a redeemer arrived to restore Catholicism's old values. The Florentines responded with enthusiasm, because the killjoy cleric had forced them to abandon their carefree carnivals. He was stretched on the rack 14 times in one day during weeks of persecution before being publicly hanged. His body was then burned.

The Pope sent his son Giovanni off with the army to attack the fortresses of the Orsini family, who had also collaborated with the French. But he proved a hopeless general and returned to Rome in disgrace early in 1497 after losing a battle against the foes he was supposed to punish. Months later, on 14 June, he dined with his mother and brother Cesare. The two men left separately on horseback. Next morning Giovanni's body was dragged from the river Tiber. He had been stabbed nine times.

Giovanni's assassin was never caught, and officially the murder remained a mystery. But wagging tongues noted that one man gained more from the death than most – younger brother Cesare. It meant he could give up the religious positions he held so reluctantly and become the Pope's political and military strong man. That was good news for the Pope, too. Rodrigo could send Cesare away from Rome on business and quell the growing clamour of scandalized gossip. The cardinal's sexual proclivities – he found young boys as alluring as girls, and was far from discreet about his flings with either sex – were the talk of the town. Most embarrassing was his continuing affair with his own sister, Lucrezia. She was placed in a convent when her first husband fled for fear of Cesare's jealous rages. But six months later, after visits from Cesare and his father, she became pregnant. The baby boy was later taken to the Vatican and made heir to the Borgia fortune.

Cesare's new duties took him first to Naples, then to France. The new French king, Louis XII, wanted to annul his marriage and wed his mistress. Rodrigo agreed. In return, Cesare was made Duke of Valentinois and given a bride, the 16-year-old sister of the King of Navarre. More importantly, he was offered French armed help to subdue rebellious nobles in northern Italy and carve out a kingdom for himself in Romagna, south of Venice. The joint invasion began in 1499.

Cesare proved as cunning and unscrupulous in war as he had proved in love. When he crushed the forces of Caterina Sforza and captured her castle at Forli, he insisted that she also surrender her body to him. He wrote a gloating description of their love-making to his father in Rome before confining her in a convent. He took the town of Faenza after stubborn resistance by a population devoted to their 18-year-old master, Astorre Manfredi. The teenager agreed to surrender only after he was promised that his life would be spared. But Cesare sent him to Rome and had him horribly tortured, then killed.

Friends and allies of Cesare had as much to fear from him as from their foes. He betrayed the trust of the Duke of Urbino, marching his men past the city, then doubling back to launch a surprise attack. He appointed a ruthless governor to rule his new lands in Romagna – but when protests about the man's cruelty became impossible to ignore, he had him hacked in two and left on display in Sesena town square. Soon even some of Cesare's lieutenants were alienated by the reign of terror imposed by their morose, unsympathetic leader. Afraid that he might reclaim estates he had given them, they began plotting against him with princes he had deposed. Cesare learned of the conspiracy and lured some of the unsuspecting plotters to a banquet at the town of Senigallia. When they arrived, unarmed, they were seized. Two were instantly strangled.

Cesare's costly campaigns were funded by the Pope. Rodrigo sold cardinal's hats to wealthy aspirants, some of whom died mysteriously only months later leaving their estates to the Vatican. He declared the year 1500 a Jubilee, which meant pilgrims prepared to pay would receive total absolution for their trespasses. As an added inducement, he announced the unveiling of a 'secret holy door' in St Peter's which was only ever revealed once every 100 years. Grateful and gullible sinners paid handsomely for the rare privilege of viewing the door, which had been cut in the wall shortly before their arrival.

Rome's death rate rose every time Cesare returned from his territorial conquests. He answered insults, real or imagined, with murder. Many of his homosexual partners were also found poisoned, or dragged from the Tiber with fatal knife wounds. The Venetian ambassador wrote: 'Every night four or five murdered men are discovered – bishops, prelates and others – so that all Rome is trembling for fear of being destroyed by the Duke Cesare.' Then, in 1500, Cesare's fiery passion for sister Lucrezia led to a sensational killing.

Rodrigo had quietly annulled his daughter's first marriage after her husband fled Cesare's jealousy. And in the wake of the scandal over Lucrezia's baby, the Pope had rushed her to the altar with Alphonse, Duke of Bisceglie and the brother of Sanchia. Sadly, Lucrezia had genuinely fallen in love with him. That infuriated Cesare, who still prefered his sister's embraces to those of his wife.

In July 1500, Alphonse was walking across St Peter's Square after sharing supper with the Pope when a gang of thugs disguised as pilgrims attacked him with knives. He survived, though seriously wounded, and was given a room near the Pope's quarters to ensure his future safety. Lucrezia nursed him devotedly. But one night, having left his bedside briefly, she returned to find him dead. Amazingly, Cesare confessed to strangling him, saying the Duke had earlier tried to murder him with a crossbow. But no action was taken. And in less than two weeks Cesare was again forcing his attentions on his grief-stricken sister. Their incestuous liaison continued until Rodrigo arranged another match for Lucrezia, with the Duke of Ferraro's son. On their last night together before she left for the nuptials, Cesare arranged a special treat in his Vatican rooms – 50 local socialites rolled naked on the floor, scrambling for hot roasted chestnuts tossed to them by the illicit lovers.

But the debauched days of the unholy Borgia alliance were numbered. In August 1503, Rodrigo and Cesare both fell ill with malaria after attending a party thrown by a cardinal in a vineyard just outside Rome. Within a week the 72-year-old Pope was dead. And Cesare, who knew that all his power derived from his father's protection, was too weak to look after his own interests.

For a while he had reason to hope that he could still maintain power. Rodrigo's successor as Pope was an ineffectual old man who bore no grudge against Cesare. But he died just one month after taking office. Unluckily for Cesare, the old man's successor was Giuliano della Rovere, who still resented his defeat by Rodrigo in the election of 1492.

Cesare was arrested and forced to relinquish his Romagna kingdom. He left Rome for Naples, then under Spanish rule, hoping to be allowed to build a new power base. Instead he was again arrested, for disturbing the peace of Italy, and taken to Spain where he spent two years in jail. In 1506 he escaped and sought sanctuary with his brother-in-law, the King of Navarre. But, on 12 March, 1507, he was wounded leading a siege of the town of Viana during a territorial dispute with Spain. His captors showed him as much mercy as he had shown his own victims – they stripped him naked and left him to die of thirst.

The Conquistadores

Christian fervour reigned in Catholic Spain in the 16th Century. The dreaded Inquisition spread its bloody tyranny, the entire Dutch people were excommunicated and an invasion armada was sent to convert Protestant England. But missionary mania was not confined to Europe. When explorers sailed home with news of distant lands across the Atlantic full of strange peoples and untold riches, armed expeditions set out to claim them for

King and Pope. Natives of the Caribbean, Mexico and Central America were conquered and tamed in the name of Christ. Then the discovery of the Pacific Ocean opened up fresh horizons.

In 1527 a Spanish galleon investigating the new sea captured a balsa raft crammed with beautiful gold and silver objects studded with precious gems. The natives crewing the raft were the first clue to an unexpected and extraordinary civilization which had prospered in total isolation from the known world – the Incas. And the cargo they carried was enough to condemn their well-ordered empire to destruction. For although Spanish conquistadores, led by Francisco Pizarro, justified their invasion as a crusade for God and the Bible, they committed every sin in the book in pursuit of their real aim – treasure.

Pizarro, illegitimate son of a soldier from Trujillo, had spent 30 years in the new world subjugating 'savages'. Though an important member of Panama's Spanish community, he had not yet found the crock of gold that would make his fortune. With seizure of the Inca raft, he saw his chance. He obtained royal permission to explore and conquer Peru. Dominican monk Friar Vicente de Valverde was to go with him as 'protector' of the Indians.

The expedition left Panama in December 1530. Pizarro established a coastal base, killing the local chief to intimidate nearby natives, then moved inland with 168 soldiers, 62 on horses. He could not have arrived at a better time for Spain. Disease had ravaged the Inca court, killing the Inca himself, Huayna-Capac, and his heir. Two more of his sons, Huascar and Atahualpa, had begun a civil war for control of the empire, which stretched 3,000 miles through Chile, Bolivia, Ecuador and south Colombia as well as Peru. The conquistadores found towns in ruins and Indian corpses dangling from trees as they pressed up into the mountains.

Atahualpa, who commanded the area of Peru where the Spanish had landed, was none too pleased when his scouts reported that the strangers were pillaging the countryside as they advanced. But he sent the conquistadores gifts and invited them to meet him at Cajamarca. His army was camped beyond the town, and Atahualpa told Pizarro's envoys he would visit their leader in the town's central square next day. But when he arrived, carried on a litter by 80 men and surrounded by thousands of unarmed natives, the conquistadores stayed hidden in the buildings around the square. Friar Valverde emerged with an interpreter, carrying a cross and a Bible, and began explaining his religion to the baffled chief. Then he handed Atahualpa the book. But the Incas did not understand writing. They worshipped the sun, and claimed their images of it spoke to them. When the pages of the Bible did not speak, Atahualpa threw the book to the ground. The furious priest screamed for the insult to be avenged – and Pizarro unleashed a brutal and carefully planned ambush.

'The Spaniards began to fire their muskets and charged upon the Indians with horses, killing them like ants,' Inca nobleman Huaman Poma told chroniclers. 'At the sound of the explosions and the jingle of bells on the horses' harnesses, the shock of arms and the whole amazing novelty of the attackers' appearance, the Indians were terror-stricken. The pressure of their numbers caused the walls of the square to crumble and fall. They were desperate to escape from being trampled by horses and in their headlong flight a lot of them were crushed to death. So many Indians were killed that it was impractical to count them.' After two hours of horrific slaughter, nearly 7,000 natives were dead and thousands more maimed by sword slashes. All 80 carriers of Atahualpa were massacred, but he himself was spared. Pizarro needed him alive as insurance for the invaders' safety until reinforcements arrived.

The captive Inca noted the conquistadores' glee as they ravaged his camp for treasure, and made a shrewd offer. He would buy his freedom by filling a room 22 feet (6.7m) long by 17 feet (5.1m) wide with treasure, to a depth of 8ft (2.4m). He would fill it once with gold and twice with silver. Pizarro accepted, promising to restore Atahualpa to his stronghold at Quito as long as he instigated no plots against the Spanish. The Inca told the invaders where to find his temples and directed a scouting party to his capital, Cuzco. It returned with 285 llamas loaded with gold and silver stripped from palaces, tombs and holy places. Other treasure trains poured in from all over the empire. Pizarro crushed jars, jugs and sculptures so the room would hold more. Then he set up furnaces to melt all the precious metals into bars. There were six tons (6,096kg) of 22 carat gold and 12 tons (12,192kg) of silver, a total then worth nearly £3 million.

Atahualpa, confident of release, had secretly continued his civil war, having his troops kill Huascar and two of his half-brothers. But all he was doing was playing into Pizarro's hands by weakening the empire's chances of ever repelling the invaders. Pizarro had no intention of letting the Inca go. Now he had Atahualpa's treasure, he planned to march on to Cuzco with recently arrived reinforcements, and could not afford to take the native leader along as a magnet for possible attacks. Rumours of an approaching Inca army, out to rescue their chief, were the excuse Pizarro needed. He sent out search parties to check the reports. But before they returned, Atahualpa was dead. Condemned without trial for treason, he was tied to a stake on 26 July, 1533, and told he would be burned alive unless he became a Christian. He agreed to be converted, taking the name Francisco in honour of Pizarro. Then he was garrotted.

The death caused a furore in Spain and its other colonies. In Madrid the King was angry that a fellow royal had been illegally executed. The governor of Panama said Atahualpa had 'done no harm to any Spaniard'. But Pizarro survived the storm. He reasoned, rightly, that the crown's one-fifth share of all booty would calm humanitarian qualms.

The march to Cuzco started uneventfully. The invaders were going through

Francisco Pizarro

Huascar country, and locals welcomed the death of Atahualpa. They were trusting, gentle people – their homes did not have doors, let alone locks – and were in awe of the magnificent appearance of the newcomers. Having never seen horses before, some thought mount and rider were one being. Others believed the armour-plated conquistadores, white-faced and wearing strange beards, heralded the return of their sun god Viracocha. They were to pay for their naïveté by losing their wealth, their land, their women, their religion – and, for thousands, their lives.

The first armed opposition to Pizarro's men came 17 months after he landed in Peru. Troops loyal to Atahualpa attacked at Jauja, 250 miles north of Cuzco. But they were trying to fight cavalry armed with pistols, lances and steel swords using only clubs, bronze axes and stone slingshots. The native forces were routed by charging horses and mercilessly pursued and cut down as they fled. When the futile ambushes continued, Pizarro burned captive commander Chulcuchima alive, accusing him of inspiring the raids. The Inca general defiantly refused to spare himself agony by becoming a Christian.

The town of Cuzco welcomed the Spanish as liberators. And Huascar's son Manco welcomed them most. He was ready to collaborate if they made him Inca. Pizarro willingly installed him, then organized systematic looting of the empire's richest city. Temple walls, priceless statues, jewels and vases buried with the dead, even a unique artificial garden of intricate golden plants, were melted down. A young priest who watched with horror wrote: 'Their only concern was to collect gold and silver to make themselves rich . . . What was being destroyed was more perfect than anything they enjoyed or possessed.' But clerical concern at the abuse of a peaceful people in the Church's name could not stop it. As the governor of Panama reported to the King: 'The greed of Spaniards of all classes is so great as to be insatiable. The more the native chiefs give, the more the Spaniards kill or torture them to give more.'

Reports of the riches available in the Inca land sparked off a gold rush in other colonies. In Puerto Rico, the governor banned anyone leaving. When he caught a boatload of would-be treasure-hunters, he flogged them and cut off their feet. But still new adventurers reached Peru, committing atrocities in the race to get rich quickly.

Pedro de Alvarado marched into northern Peru, chaining up hundreds of native porters from the tropical coastal areas and watching them die cruelly in the icy Andes. Men, women and children were killed as towns were sacked, and local chieftains were hanged, burned or thrown to dogs when, under torture, they refused to divulge the whereabouts of treasure. Sebastian de Benalcazar burned the feet of chiefs to force them to reveal treasure troves. In one village, where all the men had fled to join Inca armies, he massacred the remaining women and children because there were not enough riches to satisfy his cravings. It was 'cruelty unworthy of a Castillian', according to the official chronicler of the Peruvian conquest. Other Spaniards buried native chiefs up to their waists in pits to try to force them to give away the hiding places of gold. When they would not – or could not – they were flogged, then buried up to their necks before being killed.

Reports of cruelty flooded into Cuzco, angering the Inca Manco. He also had personal reasons to regret collaborating with the Spanish. The town was in the control of Pizzaros's brothers, Juan, Hernando and Gonzalo, after Francisco left for the coast to found the new city of Lima. The Inca was continually pestered to reveal more treasure caches. His mother and sisters were raped. Then Gonzalo stole his wife. Such humiliation of himself and his people was more than the proud prince could stand. He and his elders decided to rebel. In 1535 he slipped out of the town at night, but was recaptured by horsemen and returned in chains. Spaniards urinated on him and tortured him, burning his eyelashes with a candle. But a year later he successfully escaped, determined to make the invaders pay for treating him so disgustingly.

Manco had secretly mobilized a vast native army, and began deploying it with devastating effect. He lured Cuzco's cavalry to nearby Calca, allowing them to seize a treasure train. While they counted their plunder, thousands of natives surrounded Cuzco, diverting irrigation canals to flood fields, making them impossible for horses to operate on. It was the start of a four-month siege. Three squads of Spaniards marching to the rescue were wiped out by native ambushers, who hurled giant boulders down deep gorges to knock them off tortuous mountain paths. Spaniards in Jauja were all killed in a dawn raid. But the conquistadores hit back with subterfuge and savagery to quell the rebellion.

Four shaved off their beards and blacked their faces to appear like Indians. Then, with the help of a native traitor, they got into an inaccessible fortress and opened the gates for colleagues to run amok. Hundreds of Indians leapt to their deaths off cliffs to escape Spanish swords. Morgovejo de Quinones, riding to relieve Cuzco, decided to avenge the death of 5 Spanish travellers by herding 24 chiefs and elders of a nearby town into a thatched building, then setting light to it and burning them alive. When the encircled horsemen in Cuzco broke out to attack a native fortress – Juan Pizarro was killed by a sling stone in the raid – so many Indians leapt from the battlements that the last to jump were cheated of death because the bodies piled beneath them broke their fall. More than 1,500 natives still in the fort were put to the sword. Conquistadores led by Gonzalo Pizarro surprised an indian army and massacred the men. Those who plunged into a lake to try to escape were pursued by horsemen and 'speared like fish.'

Horror and mutilation were deliberately used by the Spanish to demoralize their foes. Hernando Pizarro ordered that all women caught near battlefields were to be killed. They were the Inca soldiers' wives and mistresses. When brother Gonzalo captured 200 Indian fighters, he paraded them in the square at Cuzco and sliced off all their right hands. Then he sent them back to their comrades as 'a dreadful warning.' Later male captives had their noses cut off. Women who escaped death had their breasts chopped. In the Huaylas area, Francisco de Chaves instituted a three-month reign of terror. Homes and fields were destroyed, men and women burned or impaled, and 600 children aged under three were slaughtered.

The final blow to Manco's hopes came when an army led by his commander Quizo tried to take Francisco Pizarro's capital, Lima. Cavalry devastated the foot soldiers as they advanced across the coastal plain, and the horsemen massacred survivors of the charge as they fled towards safety in the mountains. Quizo and 40 fellow generals were among the dead.

Manco now realized he could not save Peru from the Spanish. More than 20,000 of his people had died trying. He retreated to Vilcabamba, a desolate valley screened by misty crags, and escaped his pursuers by hiding with forest Indians. But the Spaniards caught his wife, Cura Ocllo. And Francisco Pizarro took out his anger on her. Pizarro had proved during the siege of Lima that he had no qualms about killing women. Atahualpa's sister Azarpay was his prisoner there. He suspected her of encouraging the native attackers and had her garrotted. He had an even worse fate in mind for Cura Ocllo.

The poor woman only escaped rape at the hands of her escort soldiers by smearing herself with excrement. When she reached Cuzco, where Pizarro was waiting for news of the pursuit of the Inca, she was stripped naked, tied to a stake and savagely beaten. Finally she was killed by arrow shots. Her battered body was loaded into a basket and floated on a river which flowed into Vilcabamba, so the Inca could see the fate of his spouse. It was yet another horror to appal decent-minded Spaniards. One called it 'an act totally unworthy of a sane Christian gentleman.' Sadly, such acts were becoming all too common in the conquest of Peru.

But Pizarro's days were numbered. The lure of gold had led Spaniards to fight each other. Hernando Pizarro was recalled to Spain and jailed for garrotting without trial Diego de Almagro, one of the first conquistadores, who had rebelled for a bigger share of the booty. On 26 June, 1541, Almagro's followers took revenge. Twenty of them stormed Francisco Pizarro's Lima palace and stabbed him to death. Another victim of the raid was the cruel child-killer Francisco de Chaves. Friar Vicente de Valverde, the man who had helped dupe Atahualpa, panicked at the death of his patron Pizarro and took ship for Panama. On an island off Peru, he was captured by cannibals and eaten.

Pizarro had succeeded in his quest. Contemporaries praised him for acquiring more gold and silver than any other commander the world had seen. But the religious cause which justified his exploits played little part in his epitaph. His achievements were best summed up in the coat of arms awarded him by the King of Spain when he made him a marquis. It showed seven native chiefs with chains round their necks, and a shackled Atahualpa, his hands delving into two treasure chests.

Pizarro's passing did not end the suffering his invasion inflicted on Peru. And deaths resisting his takeover accounted for just a fraction of the estimated five million drop in the empire's native population between 1530 and the end of the century. The other reasons were spelled out damningly in John Hemming's authoritative book, *The Conquest Of The Incas*. They were:

Disease: Peruvians had no immunity to European ailments such as smallpox, measles, the plague. Epidemics raged uncontrollably. The town of Quito lost 30,000 in just one.

Neglect: Preoccupied by gold and silver, the Spaniards failed to maintain precious irrigation canals, agricultural terraces, roads and bridges. Where the Incas filled communal storehouses for times of hardship, the Spanish merely looted them.

Hunger: Apart from taking the natives' precious metals, the conquistadores and their successors seized, slaughtered and sold at ridiculously cheap prices their herds of llama. Harvests were also grabbed for cheap sale.

Exploitation: Francisco Pizarro had divided the nation into vast estates. Natives living on them had to provide annual tribute – gold, silver, livestock, grain, potatoes, eggs, salt, timber, utensils, clothing – whether the land provided them or not. Get-rich-quick landlords increased their demands until many natives worked all year just to provide the tribute, with no time or energy to look after their families. Many became wandering vagabonds to escape impossible obligations.

Plantations: Indians from the snowbound Andes were herded down to humid forests to harvest lucrative crops of coca, the plant that provides cocaine. They died in their thousands from heat and coca-related diseases.

Expeditions: Greedy Spaniards followed up every rumour of another rich El Dorado, however remote the gold was said to be. Hundreds of natives were chained to act as porters. They died like flies from exhaustion, exposure or abuse.

Forced labour: Giant silver and mercury mines were set up by the Spanish, and natives from catchment areas up to 600 miles wide were forced to work them. Conscripts chipped at narrow, unsafe faces for six days at a stretch, sleeping in the fetid air of the galleries, full of acrid smoke from tallow candles which were the only lighting. Toxic gases containing arsenic added to the toll of exhaustion, heat and bad diet in the mercury mines. A monk, Domingo de Santo Tomas, called the mines 'the mouth of hell, into which a great mass of people enter every year, and are sacrificed by the greed of the Spaniards to their god.' But the carnage was too profitable to stop. The royal fifth of the annual output at the Potosi silver mine alone came to 4½ tons (4,550kg).

Yet according to John Hemming, none of these evils was the biggest killer. The main cause of death, he says, was 'profound culture shock.' The Inca people had lived without money in a benevolent welfare state which cared for them. Now, after decades of fighting, they were expected to work for cash wages by a government which cared nothing for them. Hemming quotes an Inca elder as saying: 'The Indians, seeing themselves dispossessed and robbed, allow themselves to die and do not apply themselves to anything as they did in Inca times.' They lost the will to live – and recreate. The birth rate fell as dramatically as the death toll rose.

The Madrid government tried to impose liberal laws, but the settlers rebelled – once led by Gonzalo Pizarro – insisting it was their right to exploit the land they had won as they thought fit. Rather than risk losing the flow of New World riches, the King made concessions. The exploitation went on.

The final nails in the coffin of the Inca empire were driven in by Francisco de

Toledo, who arrived as Viceroy in 1569. In two years, 1½ million natives from isolated farms and villages were forcibly uprooted and settled in towns where they were easier to convert and control. Then the Church began a drive against native religions, seizing leaders, smashing relics and rooting out rites. And the last Inca king was captured and killed.

The murder of a Spanish messenger, trying to deliver letters to the new Inca, Tupac Amaru, was the excuse Toledo needed to invade Vilcabamba, the mysterious last refuge of the Peruvian royal family. Native sticks and stones were no match for the cannons and muskets of the 250-strong Spanish force. The Inca and his generals were caught as they tried to flee through the forests, and dragged to Cuzco in chains. Tupac Amaru was accused of ruling a heathen state which allowed heathen practices and raided Spanish Peru. He was also charged with specific murders, including that of the messenger. Despite pleas for mercy from all over Peru, and despite an astonishing public admission that the Inca religion of sun worship was a sham, Tupac Amaru was beheaded in front of vast, emotional crowds. It was almost 40 years to the day since the death of his great-uncle Atahualpa.

Toledo wanted to rid Peru of all Inca influence. He married princesses to Spaniards against the girls' wills, and sentenced several relatives of Tupac Amaru to Mexican exile – a decision over-ruled by Madrid. But all his efforts were in vain. Over 200 years later, when Peruvians successfully fought for independence from Spain, one of their heroes was Jose Gabriel Condorcanqui Tupac Amaru – great-great-great-grandson of the last Inca.

Pirates: evil on the high seas

The Venetian ambassador to London, Giovanni Scaramelli, wrote to his city's Doge and senate in 1603: 'How just is the hatred which all peoples bear to the English, for they are the disturbers of the whole world. The whole strength and repute of the nation rests on its vast number of corsairs. To such a state has this unhappy kingdom come, that from a lofty religion has fallen into the abyss of infidelity.'

Scaramelli was writing home in dismay at the realization that a mighty nation had granted a licence to criminals to guard its furthest colonial frontiers and boost its revenues. Those criminals called themselves corsairs, privateers, buccaneers or, grandly, 'the brethren of the coast.' In reality, they were no more than pirates. In the service of the English Crown, carrying no-questions-asked commissions, they were seaborne merchants of death and destruction.

Since the early sixteenth century, deserters, felons and shipwrecked smugglers had been abandoned to their fate on the coasts of the Caribbean islands, mainly Cuba, Jamaica and Hispaniola. They lived off wild pigs, the meat of which they cured by smoking in long strips over wood-and-dung fires. The dried meat was known as *boucan* and the wild men of the islands were termed *boucaniers*.

Through trade with passing ships, they acquired an arsenal of weapons, which they used to good effect in raids on the ill-defended colonial outposts – mainly Spanish – then being established throughout the islands. They drank a fearsome mixture of rum and gunpowder, wore trousers of uncured rawhide and shirts stained with pigs' blood. They must have smelt revolting and looked like savages. They certainly struck fear into the hearts of the Spaniards . . . with good reason.

In the first half of the seventeenth century, these buccaneers took to the sea. They stole small boats or fashioned canoes from hollowed tree trunks and sailed out of coves to attack Spanish shipping. The buccaneers would manouevre outside the line of fire of the Spanish guns, then race in close under constant covering fire and clamber aboard the sterns of the great galleons. Captured ships would be looted and occasionally impounded into the service of the attackers. The age of the pirate was born.

With names like Roche Braziliano, Red Legs Greaves, Pierre le Grand and Montbars the Exterminator, they harried Spain's treasure fleets and repeatedly sacked her outposts in the Central American isthmus, torturing the inhabitants without mercy until they revealed their hidden hoards. Most feared among them was a Breton captain, François Lolonois.

At the head of an army of 700 men, Lolonois razed Maracaibo to the ground and rampaged through what is now Nicaragua, lining Spanish prisoners before him and slaughtering them a dozen at a time for the sheer fun of it. According to one chronicler, Lolonois once 'grew outrageously passionate in so much that he drew his cutlass, slashed open the heart of a poor Spaniard and, pulling it out, began to gnaw it, saying to the rest that he would serve them all alike if they did not talk.' Among his other delights, Lolonois would 'cut a man to pieces, first some flesh, then a hand, an arm, a leg, sometimes tying a cord about his head and with a stick twisting it till his eyes shoot out, which is called woolding.' Lolonois met a fittingly unpleasant fate himself, being torn limb from limb by Indians.

The ease with which the buccaneers were able to relieve the Spanish of the gold they had themselves stolen from the natives of central and south America ushered in a new and, if anything, even bloodier age of piracy. For, under the guise of a crusade against Popery, Britain entered the arena and effectively gave its citizens a free hand in ravaging, robbing and persecuting neighbouring colonies with whom they were not even at war. These sea-going criminals were issued with commissions which were no more than licences to kill.

Foremost amongst them was Henry Morgan, a farmer's son born in Llanrhymney, Glamorgan. How he got to the West Indies is not known. He may have been transported, he may have been an indentured servant or he may have arrived in 1655 with Oliver Cromwell's army. In 1663 his uncle, Sir Edward Morgan, was appointed Deputy Governor-General of Jamaica and, although there is no evidence, it is likely that this valuable family connection helped the young Welshman launch his piratical career. For Jamaica's Government House was the principal source of buccaneers' commissions, handed out freely under the guise of guarding the colony against Spanish 'invasion'. In return for the commissions, the governor, the notoriously corrupt planter Sir Thomas Modyford, and his deputy received their own 'commission' – a share in the pirate plunder.

First records of Morgan's activities date from 1665 when he was involved in skirmishes with the Spanish in Costa Rica. Two years later, despite a British peace treaty with Spain, Modyford authorized Henry Morgan to assemble a fleet of 12 ships and to sweep the Spanish colonies for booty.

Morgan fast gained a reputation for barbarity. In Puerto del Principe, Cuba, he systematically tortured the townspeople until he was satisfied no hidden treasures remained. Then he sailed south to the Panama isthmus where he launched an ambitious attack on the impressively fortified town of Portobello. His men scaled the walls of the town by forcing captured priests and nuns up the scaling ladders as a human shield.

Morgan's savage rampage almost came to an early end in 1669 when, about to raid Maracaibo, he called all his captains and senior officers to a council of war aboard his flagship, the *Oxford*, in Port Royal harbour. Midway through the discussions, the *Oxford* was torn apart by an explosion in the powder magazine. Two hundred men, including five captains, died. Among the council of war, only Morgan and 25 others survived – watching horrified as everyone on the opposite side of a chart table was blown to bits. Morgan was unharmed but his reputation was dented.

The following year Morgan determined to restore his prestige and to ensure riches that would last him a lifetime by carrying out a single, dramatic raid on the richest city of the west. He planned to attack 'the Cup of Gold' – Panama City itself.

In 1670, ignoring yet another newly signed treaty between Spain and Britain,

Henry Morgan assembled more than 2,000 men and 36 ships, victualled his fleet by sacking a dozen or more townships and set sail for Panama. En route he stopped at Providence Island where the governor agreed to surrender if Morgan staged a mock attack using gunpowder but no ammunition. This charade over and the garrison town sacked, the fleet sailed to the mouth of the River Chagre, which breaches the Darien isthmus, and took the sentinel Fort San Lorenzo with the loss of 100 buccaneers.

The city of Panama was only 50 miles away but they were 50 miles of disease-ridden swamp and dense jungle inhabited by unfriendly natives. After five days his men, starving and shot at by Indians, urged him to turn back and relaunch the attack with greater supplies. Morgan refused. The Spanish withdrew before them, burning villages and leaving the pirates without food or fresh water. The invaders ate cats, dogs and their own leather bags before, on the tenth day, they reached Panama, routed the defenders on the plains outside the city and burned it to the ground.

The looting of Panama and the murder, rape and torture of its inhabitants produced an unrecorded fortune. But the men who had gone through hell for Henry Morgan got little reward. Morgan claimed that the booty had been far less than expected – and accordingly gave his men pathetically small hand-outs for their sacrifices. Even the widows of those who had died in his service were cheated of their agreed recompense by Morgan. The only people satisfied with the share-out were the expedition's principal backers, some of the captains . . . and Morgan himself.

Rich and famous, he was ordered to England by King Charles II to serve a period of so-called 'detention' for what was known as 'the crime of Panama'. It was no more than a feint to appease the angry Spanish. Morgan spent two years in London, a hero feted by society, before returning in 1674 to Jamaica as Sir Henry Morgan, Lieutenant-Governor, plantation owner and justice of the peace. As such, he sat in judgement on many pirates and sentenced them to prison, and to death, without mercy – this, despite his own continuing financial links with the pirate trade. He died a rich man in 1688.

The lessons in terror and barbarity of François Lolonois and Henry Morgan were well learned by pirates who followed them in the early years of the eighteenth century. Monstrous Edward Teach (better known as Blackbeard) was a sadistic psychotic who ravaged the West Indies and America's eastern seaboard under the protection of North Carolina's corrupt governor. Dashing, dandified Bartholomew 'Black Bart' Roberts was reported to have treated prisoners with 'barbarous abuse . . . some almost whipped to death, others had their ears cut off, others fixed to yardarms and fired at as a mark'.

But the pirates' crimes often seem in restrospect to have been overshadowed by a more insidious evil – on the part of the corrupt, greedy authorities who not

Henry Morgan, pirate king

Captain Kidd, before the House of Commons

only tolerated but encouraged pirate activities.

The example of royal duplicity and hypocrisy displayed by Charles II and his loyal servant Henry Morgan was exceeded by their immediate successors: King William III and a New York-based privateer called Captain Kidd. In 1695 the king granted 'to our trusty and well-beloved William Kidd' two commissions, one to seize French shipping and the other to subdue piracy (a euphemism for the confiscation of booty from other privateers). For this the king expected a 'commission' of his own of 10 per cent of the haul. After Kidd's share, the remainder would go to the expedition's backers – a syndicate of bankers, peers and Whig politicians including the Lord Chancellor and the First Lord of the Admiralty.

Kidd little needed the adventure or the money. Born in Greenock, Scotland in 1645, the son of a Presbyterian minister, he had already made his mark and his fortune as a privateer against the French in the West Indies. He had then settled in New York, married a wealthy widow and retired to a mansion in Wall Street. It was only his wish to give evidence to a British Board of Trade inquiry about the corrupt practices of an arch enemy, New York's Governor Benjamin Fletcher, that brought Kidd to London and to the attention of the king.

In 1696 Kidd, duly commissioned, sailed from England to New York, where he recruited a crew from among pirates who had once worked for Governor Fletcher. He then sailed south, around the Cape of Good Hope to the Indian Ocean, on a buccaneering rampage that brought protests from almost every major maritime nation. The British government were forced to tear up his royal commissions and order his capture. Dismayed when he heard the news, Kidd fled to the West Indies, lost most of his plunder to mutinous crews and ended up in Boston, throwing himself upon the mercy of the authorities.

The man who had the power of life or death over Kidd at that stage was the new Governor of New York, the Earl of Bellomont. The noble Earl had got the job with the help of Kidd's evidence against his predecessor. He had also been one of the secret backers of Kidd's expedition. Yet Bellomont had the captain clapped in irons and thrown into a dungeon for six months before sending him back to Britain to stand trial. Bellomont meanwhile appropriated the £14,000 which was all that Kidd had left of his haul from the South Seas.

On 23 May 1701, drunk and insensible, William Kidd was hanged at Wapping and his body suspended in chains 'to serve as a greater terror to all persons from committing the like crimes'.

François Lolonois and Henry Morgan were among the most pitiless, brutal, bloodthirsty pirates who ever put to sea – but the unfortunate Captain Kidd was very different. Though his actions were certainly criminal, the real evil was displayed by those who, to line their own pockets, secretly and hypocritically authorized piracy and murder . . . and who, when their plot began to rebound on them, covered their traces by sending the instrument of their greed to the gallows. They were men like the duplicitous New York governor and Irish peer, the Earl of Bellomont; the Lord Chancellor, Sir John Somers; the First Lord of the Admiralty, Edward Russell, later Earl of Orford; the Master of Ordnance, the Earl of Romney; Secretary of State, the Duke of Shrewsbury – and the king himself, William III.

As Kidd told the judge at his trial: 'It is a very hard sentence. I am the innocentest person of them all, only I have been sworn against by perjured persons'. It was his last appeal to those evil men in high office – and it went unheeded.

Marat and Robespierre: evil in the name of Liberty

Hailing the almost-bloodless start of the French Revolution, Honoré Gabriel Riqueti, Comte de Mirabeau, said in May 1789: 'History has too often recounted the actions of nothing more than wild animals . . . Now we are given hope that we are beginning the history of man.' But, within five years, that hope had been wiped out by one of the world's worst outbreaks of mass murder. Frenchmen freed by negotiation from almost-feudal tyranny turned into brutal, barbaric beasts on the pretext of achieving liberty, equality and fraternity. And the most poignant epitaph for Mirabeau's dream was the anguished cry of a fallen revolutionary as she was led to the guillotine: 'Oh liberty, what crimes are committed in your name.'

The Revolution erupted when public patience with the King's absolute power to impose taxes and laws ran out. Louis XVI and the privileged nobility were forced to make concessions to democracy and individual freedom. But each concession merely made the increasingly strong citizens greedy for more. 'The difficulty is not to make a revolution go, it is to hold it in check,' said Mirabeau shortly before his death in 1791. For as the people realized they had the power of life or death, negotiation was abandoned for naked force. After the storming of the Bastille, symbol of the old regime's authority, revolutionaries advocating cautious progress were drowned by the clamour of radical factions urging war on France's neighbours and dissidents at home. Then a more sinister voice demanded massacres.

Jean-Paul Marat was not even French – his father came from Sardinia, his mother was Swiss. But when the Revolution began, he abandoned his career as a scientist and doctor to become one of Paris's most vitriolic pamphleteers. His early extremism was unpopular, and several times he was forced into hiding. Once, when he took refuge in the city sewers, he contracted a painful and unpleasant skin disease, which added to his bitter persecution complex. But as the mob became increasingly impatient with a Revolution which seemed to be doing nothing to reduce raging inflation and food shortages, and with leaders who were prevaricating over the fate of Louis and his hated Austrian wife Marie Antoinette, Marat's messages began to find a receptive audience. And he spoke with chilling clarity. 'In order to ensure public tranquility,' he wrote, '200,000 heads must be cut off.'

On 10 August, 1791, an armed procession of 20,000 Parisians marched towards the royal residence, the Tuileries. The King and Queen, and their two children, were smuggled out by elected representatives and taken to the National Assembly building for protection. The Palace's Swiss Guards held the mob at bay until their ammunition ran out. They surrendered – but the mob was in no mood for mercy. More than 500 soldiers were slaughtered with pikes, bayonets, swords and clubs. Another 60 were massacred as they were marched away as captives. Palace staff, even cooks, maids and the royal children's tutor, were slashed to pieces as the Parisians ran riot. Bodies were strewn in rooms and on staircases. The grounds were littered with corpses. And onlookers were sickened to see children playing with decapitated heads. Women, 'lost to all sense of shame, were committing the most indecent mutilations on the dead bodies, from which they tore pieces of flesh and carried them off in triumph.'

The hideous orgy of blood lust instantly brought fears of a backlash from royalists or counter-revolutionaries. Marat had the answer. Many opponents of the Revolution were already packed in the jails of Paris, and might break out to seek revenge. 'Let the blood of the traitors flow,' wrote Marat. 'That is the only way to save the country.' Hysteria was whipped up by pamphlets warning of a plot to assassinate all good citizens in their beds. In September, the good citizens took steps to make that impossible.

A party of priests who had refused to take a new vow severing their allegiance to Rome were being escorted to prison in six carriages. A mob ambushed them, plunging swords through the carriage windows to wound and mutilate indiscriminately. Then, at the gates of the jail, another mob was waiting. When the convoy arrived, and the priests tried to dash inside for safety, they were slaughtered. Soon afterwards, a bunch of thugs burst into a convent where 150 more priests were being held, along with an archbishop. He was stabbed first. Then the others were killed in pairs, their bodies thrown down a well.

Over the next week, gangs broke into jails, prison hospitals and mental asylums all over Paris, massacring inmates with swords, axes and iron bars. Only prisons for prostitutes and debtors were spared. Women were on hand with food and drink for the executioners. Drunken killers held mock trials for some of the victims. One woman awaiting trial for mutilating her lover had her breasts cut off and her feet nailed to the floor before being burned alive. Marie Thérèse de Savoie-Carignan, Princesse de Lamballe, a friend of Marie Antoinette, was stripped and raped. Then her body was ripped to pieces. A leg was stuffed into a cannon, her head was stuck on a pole, and her heart cut out, roasted and eaten.

Ghastly scenes of grisly glee were reported as the piles of corpses built up. Drunken women sat watching the debauched death-dealers, laughing and applauding at each new depravity. Some pinned cut-off ears to their skirts as gruesome souvenirs. Others drank aristocratic blood handed round by the killers, or dipped bread in it. Men sat on bloodied bodies, smoking and joking while they rested from their labours. In six days, during which the gutters ran red, half the prison population, nearly 1,200 people, were murdered. And those who took a day off work to join the extermination squads were paid compensation for lost wages by delighted leaders of the Paris Commune.

The excesses appalled many of the most radical revolutionaries. But Marat was unrepentant. He signed a letter sent by the Commune to its counterparts in provincial towns, explaining that the 'act of justice' was 'indispensable in order to restrain by intimidation the thousands of traitors hidden within our walls.' And the letter went on: 'We do not doubt that the whole nation will be anxious to adopt this most necessary method of public security; and that all Frenchmen will exclaim, with the people of Paris, "We are marching against the foe, but we will not leave these brigands behind us to cut the throats of our children and wives."' Republicans in many towns took that as their cue to match the capital's atrocities by massacring the inmates of their own jails.

In January 1793, the Revolution reached the point of no return. The elected national assembly, now called the Convention, unanimously condemned Louis XVI to death for trying to 're-establish tyranny on the ruins of liberty.' He was executed in the Place de la Révolution, formerly the Place de Louis XV. Within weeks, every major country in Europe had declared war on France, and civil war raged as peasants resisted compulsory call-up to the armed forces.

Minister of Justice Charles Danton set up a Revolutionary Tribunal to try to maintain order and avoid atrocities like the September massacres. 'Let us be terrible to prevent the people from being terrible,' he thundered. But Convention moderates believed the people would stay terrible as long as Marat was free to incite them. They ordered he be tried by the Tribunal. To their consternation, he was cleared. Carried back to the parliament in triumph by the mob, he forced through a decree ordering the arrest of 22 of his accusers.

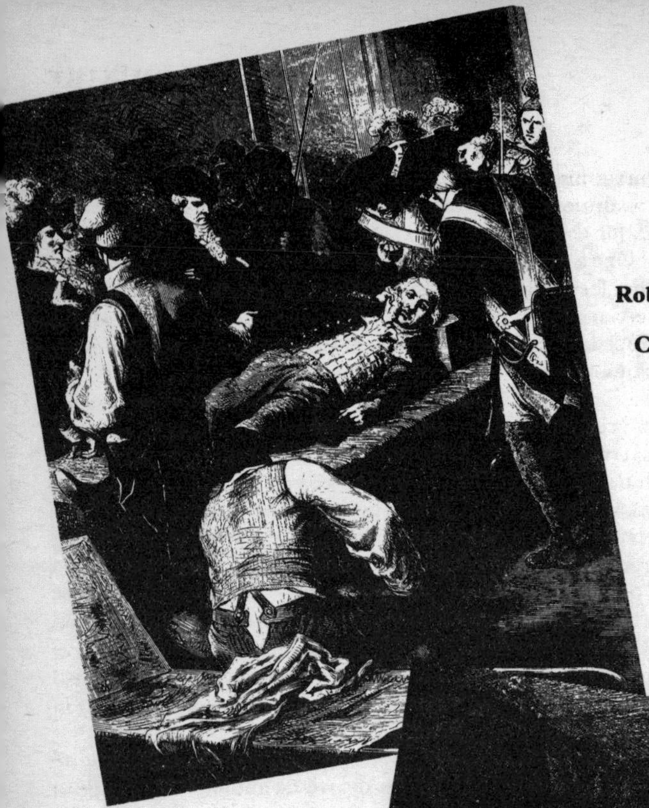

Robespierre, shot in the jaw as Convention troops arrest him

Marat discovered in his bath, with murderer Charlotte Corday beside him

Marat did not savour his victory for long. On 13 July, 1793, he was at home, wrapped in towels in a copper bath to ease the pain of his skin affliction, when a young girl arrived, claiming to know of moderates who were plotting an anti-leftist coup against Marat's party. 'They will all soon be guillotined,' Marat assured her as he jotted down the names. But the girl, Charlotte Corday, was not what she seemed. She suddenly drew a knife from her cleavage and stabbed Marat. He fell dying as aides manhandled Charlotte to the ground. She seemed oblivious to their blows. 'The deed is done,' she shouted. 'The monster is dead.'

But once again the moderates had miscalculated. Marat the monster became the mob's martyr. All over France, streets and squares were named after him. More than 30 towns changed their name to his. And his death did not divert the Revolution from the path of blood. For an even more evil man had taken over leadership of the lethal extremists, a man prepared to sacrifice even the parents of his godson at the altar of his ambitions.

Maximilien Robespierre, a cold, humourless barrister from Arras, was despised by many of his fellow revolutionaries for his fastidious appearance and his squeamishness at the sight of bloodshed. Yet by 1793 the dapper lawyer who shunned public executions because they corrupted the human soul was the most feared man in France. And he used his power, as chief of the ironically named Committee of Public Safety, to institute one of the most cruel reigns of terror in history.

Robespierre's committee directed the Revolutionary Tribunal in eradicating enemies of the republic. France was still in danger of invasion by its European neighbours, and Robespierre could justify early severity on those grounds. He ruled that all foreign nationals not living in France on 14 July, 1789 – the day the Bastille was stormed – should be arrested. And he executed the most famous foreigner on French soil – Austrian-born Queen Marie Antoinette. Charges against her included conspiracy with her brother, the Austrian Emperor, and incest with her son. Though she denied them all, she followed her husband to the guillotine on 16 October, 1793.

Soon the dreaded tumbrils were speeding almost daily to the scaffold in the Place de la Révolution bringing new victims. Pierre Vergniand, former president of the Revolutionary parliament, had warned: 'It is to be feared that the Revolution, like Saturn, will end up by devouring its own children.' Now his prophecy was coming true. He was among 20 moderates accused and condemned to death at a show trial. One stabbed himself to death in the courtroom with a concealed dagger – but his lifeless body accompanied his luckless colleagues for ritual decapitation next day.

More than 3,000 Parisians followed them to the blade. They included former royal mistress Madame Du Barry, accused of mourning the executed king while she was in London; a general who 'surrounded himself with aristocratic officers and never had good republicans at his table'; an innkeeper who 'furnished to the defenders of the country sour wine injurious to health'; a gambler who insulted patriots during a card game dispute; and a man who rashly shouted 'Vive le Roi' after a court jailed him for 12 years for another offence. Author Christopher Hibbert, in his authoritative book *The French Revolution*, says alleged speculators and hoarders died for 'starving the people' and one man paid the penalty 'for not giving his testimony properly.'

Vast crowds watched the executions, eating, drinking and laying bets on the order in which each batch of victims would lose their heads. English writer William Hazlitt reported: 'The shrieks of death were blended with the yell of the assassin and the laughter of buffoons. Whole families were led to the scaffold for no other crime than their relationship; sisters for shedding tears over the death of their brothers; wives for lamenting the fate of their husbands; innocent peasant girls for dancing with Prussian soldiers; and a woman giving suck . . . for merely saying, as a group were being conducted to slaughter, "Here is much blood shed for a trifling cause."'

The Place de la Révolution guillotine was so busy that, according to author Hibbert, people living in nearby Rue Saint-Honoré – ironically the street where Robespierre had lodgings – complained that the smell of stale blood from the stones was a health hazard and lowered the value of their houses.

Outside Paris, the vicious purges were even worse. 'The whole country seemed one vast conflagration of revolt and vengeance,' wrote Hazlitt. More than 14,000 people died as sadists and butchers in positions of office in the provinces made the most of Robespierre's instructions. Others killed to keep up with them, afraid they might be labelled weak or counter-revolutionaries. At Lyons, the Committee of Public Safety mowed down 300 convicted prisoners with a cannon. At Bordeaux a woman who wept when her husband was guillotined was forced to sit beneath the blade while his blood dripped on to her. Then she too was beheaded.

At Nantes, Jean-Baptiste Carrier was busy earning himself immortality as one of the worst brutes in the annals of infamy. Mass-killer Carrier, a lawyer like Robespierre, found the guillotine too slow for his taste. He packed victims into barges, towed them to the middle of the river Loire, then drowned them. Some couples were stripped naked and strapped together, face to face. Men waited with hatchets on the shore, to make sure no one got away. More than 2,000 people died in the river. Ships setting sail brought corpses up with their anchors, and the water became so polluted that catching fish in it was banned.

Carrier was also a child-killer. The guillotine was unsatisfactory – tiny heads were chopped in half because the necks made too small a target for the blade. And one executioner collapsed and died from the trauma of beheading four little sisters. So Carrier had 500 children taken to fields outside the town, where they were shot and cudgelled to death. But disease cheated the butcher of some of his prey. An epidemic swept through his overcrowded prisons, killing 3,000 inmates.

Millions of Frenchmen lived in terror of the midnight knock on the door that spelt arrest. Robespierre's spies were everywhere, and his assistants ensured that the pace of persecution never slackened. 'Liberty must prevail at any price,' declared Louis de Saint-Just, nicknamed Robespierre's Angel of Death. 'We must rule by iron those who cannot be ruled by justice,' he ordered. 'You must punish not merely traitors, but the indifferent as well.'

Early in 1794 Robespierre arrested more than 20 Convention members suspected of being critical of the way their Revolution was going. One of them was Camille Desmoulins. Robespierre was godfather to his son, but that made no difference. Desmoulins had said: 'Love of country cannot exist when there is neither pity nor love for one's fellow countrymen, but only a soul dried up and withered by self-adulation.' He named no names, but everyone knew who his target was. Saint-Just hit back: 'A man is guilty of a crime against the republic when he takes pity on prisoners. He is guilty because he has no desire for virtue.' Desmoulins died – and so did his 23-year-old widow, because she appealed to Robespierre for mercy.

Danton, too, was among this consignment of children of the Revolution to be devoured. Robespierre had decided that the notorious womanizer could never be a fit champion of freedom. Danton confided to friends that he would not fight his accuser, because 'far too much blood has been shed already.' He added: 'I had the Revolutionary Tribunal set up. I pray to God and men to forgive me for it.'

With his main potential rivals purged, Robespierre again stepped up the slaughter. The Committee of Public Safety decreed that death was henceforth the only sentence it would impose. Defence lawyers, witnesses and preliminary investigations were all banned, and an official said: 'For a citizen to become suspect, it is now sufficient that rumour accuses him.' Hundreds more aristocrats were executed – 1,300 in Paris in one month alone. 'At the point we are now, if we stop too soon we will die,' Robespierre told the Convention. 'Freedom will be extinguished tomorrow.'

But in the Convention, more and more delegates shared Danton's belated repugnance at the killings – and, at last, summoned the courage to resist Robespierre. For 24 hours the Convention was split, with both sides drawing up indictments to arrest their opponents. Finally, the vote went against Robespierre, Saint-Just and 18 of their closest associates. But in the confusion, troops detailed to escort Robespierre to jail proved loyal to him, and installed him in a safe house. The Convention summoned more soldiers to recapture him. When they burst in, a shot smashed Robespierre's jaw. Next day, 28 July, 1794, he was in agony as the Revolutionary Tribunal he had used so lethally sentenced him and his aides to death. Hours later, the tumbrils took all the arrested men to the guillotine, pausing momentarily outside Robespierre's lodgings while a boy smeared blood from a butcher's shop on the door. Robespierre was the last to die. When his turn came, a woman screamed at him: 'You monster spewed out of hell, go down to your grave burdened with the curses of the wives and mothers of France.'

The new Revolutionary regime revenged itself on Robespierre's followers. Many were executed after trials – Carrier was guillotined on 16 November – and hundreds more were lynched in jails all over the country. The people's revolution was at last over.

The French had paid a bloody price for allowing the likes of Marat and Robespierre to lead them towards their dream of liberty, equality and fraternity.

Rev. Jim Jones

It is just possible that the Reverend Jim Jones set out to be a loving religious leader who would champion the cause of the poor and the oppressed.

Certainly, thousands of sincere worshippers, inspired by his message of brotherhood and justice, flocked to join his faithful congregation. Politicians and civic leaders hailed Jones as a selfless, tireless worker whose personal sacrifices pointed the way towards building a better society for millions in the United States.

But somewhere along the line, it all went grotesquely wrong.

Jones changed from Good Shepherd to tyrant, from benign pastor to brutal torturer. In the end he led nearly 1,000 of his followers into a nightmare in a tropical jungle in South America with the promise of building them a paradise on earth. And when concerned relatives began to plead for an investigation into the plight of the faithful in the jungle settlement of Jonestown, he had the inquiring visitors assassinated to stop them telling the outside world the truth about the living hell he had created in the name of social progress and humanity.

As his religious empire came crashing down under the weight of the terrible suffering he had inflicted on his own followers, he ordered them to commit mass suicide.

Chanting and singing his praises, elderly women and young couples cheerfully drank the deadly arsenic potion of 'holy water' he offered them. Loving parents fed their children a sweet mixture of poison and lemonade. And for those whose nerve failed them, the elders of Jones's church were ready to slit their throats or put a .38 bullet in their heads. The whole congregation died.

Jim Warren Jones was born on 13 May, 1931 in the small farming town of Lynn, Indiana, and he was doomed to grow up a lonely child. His father was a World War One veteran who suffered a disabling lung disease and who could only contribute a meagre Government pension towards the support of his family. Embittered and partly crippled, he reserved most of his strength for the fiery rallies of his favourite political cause, the racist Klu Klux Klan.

Jones's mother, Lynetta, was forced to take a factory job to make ends meet. As an adult, Jones was to claim that she was a full-blooded Cherokee Indian. Certainly he took his dark complexion and handsome features from her. And it was obvious from an early age he felt compelled to spread a different message from that of his father's racial hatred. Only an average student at school, he showed an unusual zeal for Bible studies. While his schoolmates demonstrated their energy on the football field, the Jones boy would stand on the porch of the family's run-down home and preach sermons at passers-by.

In 1949, at the age of 18, he took a part-time job as a hospital porter in nearby Richmond to support himself through religious studies at Indiana University. He also married hospital nurse Marceline Baldwin, four years his senior. The following year, although not yet an ordained minister, he became a pastor at a church in Indianapolis and helped to run its racially integrated youth centre.

For the next ten years, Jones suffered abuse at the hands of Indiana's racial bigots. Even the more conservative members of the church where he served protested about his plans to welcome black worshippers into their midst. Eventually Jones quit, but not before he had learned a valuable lesson about human behaviour. Members of the congregation who had only been lukewarm about their young pastor had closed ranks and rallied round him when Jones was attacked by outsiders. The message was clear: even people who don't enthusiastically share each other's beliefs can become loyally bound together if they feel threatened by a common enemy.

With money from his followers he eventually bought his own church, grandly named The People's Temple, in a run-down part of Indianapolis which had changed from a poor white area to a black ghetto. He preached racial integration and equality, not because it was fashionable, but because he honestly believed in it.

He and his wife adopted seven children, black, white and Asian. Boasting of his mother's Cherokee blood, he called himself 'biracial'.

Now that his new parish was to consist mainly of black churchgoers, he set out to study the style and technique of black preachers who commanded rapturous devotion from their flocks. And in Philadelphia he watched one black preacher who held his congregation absolutely spellbound. Father Divine was a hellfire-and-damnation orator, faith healer and showman who lived a life of luxury on the offerings of totally trusting followers who even believed his claims to be able to raise the dead. Jones was enthralled – and decided to test the level of allegiance of his own churchgoers.

Overnight the campaign of racist abuse against him mysteriously reached a sinister climax. He claimed he had been concussed when a Klan member smashed a bottle in his face on his doorstep. A stick of dynamite thrown into his garden caused a tremendous explosion but no damage or injuries. Newspaper reports, based mainly on information supplied by Jones himself, told of how he bravely stood up to the threats against himself and his family.

In recognition of his courageous stand, the mayor of Indianapolis appointed Jones to a £3,000-a-year job on the city's Human Rights Commission. And his congregation, feeling their young pastor to be beleaguered, gave him their unswerving devotion. Jones decided the time had come to weld the congregation even more tightly together with a common fear that was more terrifying than the threat of racism.

In 1960, when the country was going through 'nuclear war fever', millions of worried Americans built backyard nuclear fallout shelters. A popular magazine ran a tongue-in-cheek article, claiming to be a scientific survey of the 'ten safest places to live in the event of nuclear war'. Jones seized on the idea as a perfect trial of how thoroughly he could rule the lives of his followers. Two of the safest 'bolt-holes' from nuclear destruction were reported by the magazine to be Belo Horizonte in Brazil and the rural backwoods of Ukiah in California, 120 miles north of San Francisco.

The Rev. Jones suddenly announced to his church members that he had experienced 'a personal vision of the nuclear holocaust' and he told them they should be prepared to follow him to distant pastures to escape. Leaving abruptly with his family, at church expense, for a visit to Brazil, he ordered them to be ready to sell up their homes and withdraw their savings from their banks.

Jones returned from his South American trip unimpressed by Brazil but curiously interested in the prospects of the tiny, newly independent country of Guyana where he had stopped over for a few days. The former British colony, now a left-wing socialist republic, fulfilled many of his dreams of social justice, he told his congregation. As an afterthought he added that his terrible premonition of the nuclear holocaust had receded for the time being.

Emboldened and flattered by the number of devotees who had already put their homes up for sale just because of his 'premonition', Jones decided the option of fleeing from civilization should be held for a future emergency. If they

The Rev. Jim Jones

believed in him enough to let his fantasies rule their lives, he reckoned, they would believe in just about anything he told them. Now was the ideal time to launch himself into the lucrative faith-healing market.

The healing services were spectacular, profitable and fraudulent. In a religious frenzy, Jones would pass among the 'sick' and 'crippled' newcomers to his church, laying his hands on them. Selected patients would then leap joyously to their feet saying their injuries and diseases had been totally cured.

But when Jones's inner circle of church officials began to claim that he had raised forty followers from the dead, newspapers and the State Board of Psychology began to take a close interest.

The time had come to make a quick move before the press and local authorities began to pry too deeply. The ideal bolt-hole proved to be in California's Redwood Valley, near Ukiah, one of the so-called 'nuclear safe zones'.

California of the mid-sixties provided the perfect camouflage for the People's Temple. The arrival of three hundred religious enthusiasts preaching love and peace blended in neatly with a culture which had more than its fair share of 'flower children', 'peaceniks' and hippy communes.

For his so-called People's Temple to grow and flourish it only remained for Jones to convert the two potential troublemakers, civic busybodies and the press, into allies. He succeeded almost overnight. Temple members who became hard-working shop assistants and farm labourers were always the first to volunteer to work long unpaid hours organizing local charities. The church-goers acted as foster parents to take in scores of problem children from orphanages. Jones himself wooed local politicians until he was elected as foreman of the county grand jury and a director of free legal aid services.

Jones now had hundreds of supporters whose regard for him had been cleverly nurtured from respect to allegiance, from devotion to mindless blind loyalty. One shortcut for him to bring about social justice, he explained to them, was to work tirelessly in elections and canvassing to get him more political power – and to hand over most of their earnings to him.

With the dollars pouring in and the People's Temple a respectable state-registered, tax-exempt, religious organization with the worthiest ideals, he was ready for the big-time.

Jones and his flock left the backwoods for the bright lights of San Francisco. Their reputation as an industrious band of do-gooders quickly followed them as Jones set up a new Temple in downtown San Francisco. The membership swelled to 7,500.

City officials, impressed by Jones's boundless energy and his flair for organization, soon turned over to him part of their welfare programme and his Temple took over the task of dispensing thousands of free hot meals in their dining hall every day. No one realized that among the grateful recipients of the meals were many of Jones's own followers who had handed over to him their wages, their savings and even their social security payments.

In 1976 a naïve local political worker who feared an embarrassingly small turnout at a meeting for Rosalynn Carter, wife of presidential candidate Jimmy, asked Jones for help to swell the numbers at the election rally. Jones packed the hall with his supporters and received a standing ovation from the crowd. The next day the papers ran his photograph with Rosalynn Carter and when Jimmy was duly elected, Jones received an invitation to the presidential inauguration in Washington.

In the eyes of the local community he was a pillar of respectability. He openly boasted about funnelling hundreds of thousands of dollars from his Temple funds to South America to aid starving children in Guyana.

But the first defectors from his Temple began to tell a different story. They spoke of Jones's long tirades about sex during his sermons and how he demanded that happily married couples should be forced to divorce each other and remarry partners he had chosen for them among his inner circle of church elders.

They revealed how Jones insisted that, as their spiritual leader, he had the right to have sex with any woman or girl in the congregation and how he forced them to submit to his sexual demands.

They gave details of how browbeaten Temple members were made to confess publicly to imagined sins of homosexuality. And they revealed how young children were cruelly beaten on a platform in the Temple by Jones to 'make them show respect'. Young girls were made to take part in 'boxing matches', outnumbered by teams of bigger, stronger opponents who knocked them senseless. Other children vanished into a private room to meet 'the blue-eyed monster'. No sounds of beatings came from the room, only the screams of the young victims and the crackling noise of an electric cattle prod which sent surges of high voltage electricity through their bodies.

And all the time, hundreds of thousands of dollars poured into the Temple funds.

Many San Francisco newspapers had been the proud winners of hefty cash bonuses from Jones through his Temple awards for 'outstanding journalistic contributions to peace and public enlightenment'. Even the local police department had benefitted from his generous donations to the widows and orphans of officers killed in the line of duty.

There was a deep sense of disappointment in the highest circles, even up to the level of President Carter in the White House, that Jones the civic hero might just be a vicious crackpot.

As the bubble began to burst, Jones put into action his escape plan. The millions of dollars he had salted away in Guyana had already been put to use buying a lease on 20,000 acres of jungle and swamp near Port Kaituma on the country's Caribbean coast. A pavilion had been built as headquarters of 'Jonestown' and dormitories were ready for a thousand followers to join Jones in setting up a 'new, just, socialist society'.

Amazingly, a thousand loyal volunteers did go with him to Jonestown in November 1977 and San Francisco's politicians breathed a sigh of relief that a growing scandal had removed itself 2,000 miles from their doorstep. But they reckoned without the tenacity of one tough, independently-minded Congressman who wasn't prepared to leave the scandal uncovered.

Fifty-three-year-old Leo Ryan was a politician who believed in confronting problems first-hand. He had left the comfort and safety of his plush Congress office to spend time in the solitary confinement cell of Folsom Prison, California's toughest maximum security jail, to see for himself the treatment of prisoners. And he had worked undercover as a teacher in ghetto schools to expose failures in the education system.

When worried constituents told him they feared many of their loved ones – husbands and wives, sons and daughters – had discovered the truth about Jones in Guyana but were held there against their will, Ryan pressured the U.S. State Department to force a reluctant Guyanese government to allow him to fly to Jonestown to speak to Temple members himself.

Accompanied by a group of newspaper and television reporters, he arrived by chartered plane at the settlement on 17 November 1978 and walked straight into the lion's den. Jones himself was holding court in Jonestown's central pavilion. Locked away in a strongroom at the rear were 1,000 American passports which he had taken from his followers. Armed guards patrolled the outskirts of the remote settlement – 'to keep away bandits', Jones explained to the Congressman. Settlement pioneers were gaunt and hungry but most of them appeared to be still fanatically devoted to Jones.

Ryan was characteristically blunt. Addressing a meeting of the worshippers, under the gaze of the Jonestown armed guards, he explained: 'I am sure there are some of you who think this is the best thing that has ever happened to you in your lives.' He was drowned in a crescendo of shouting and cheering. 'But I promise if any of you want to leave you can come with me under my personal guarantee of protection.'

There was sullen silence.

Jones was seething. Any defectors who left with the Congressman would tell the truth about Jonestown as soon as they were away from the power of his evil spell. The façade cracked a little when one volunteer stepped forward.

That night Ryan was allowed to stay in Jonestown to talk to the settlers. The party of journalists was sent packing, to stay in Port Kaituma, six miles away. When they got there, TV reporter Don Harris reached into his pocket for a note which had been secretly thrust into his hand in Jonestown. It bore four names and the plaintive cry for help: 'Please, please get us out of here before Jones kills us'.

The following day when the journalists returned, Ryan was waiting for them with 20 terrified worshippers who wanted to leave. One by one Jones hugged them as they lined up to ride in an earth-moving truck through the jungle to the airstrip. But there were too many of them for the small plane to carry in one trip and Ryan bravely volunteered to stay behind until the plane could make a second journey.

Then there was a scuffle and a spurt of blood, followed by a grisly cheer. One of Jones's elders had pulled a knife and accidentally slashed himself as he tried to stab Ryan. The journalists pulled the blood-stained Congressman aboard the truck and roared away towards the airfield. They were still trembling beside the runway, briefing the pilot, when a tractor drove through the undergrowth on to the concrete. A volley of shots rang out from the men on the tractor. Ryan was killed instantly, his face blown off. Don Harris, the TV reporter, died as he took the full force of a blast from an automatic rifle. His cameraman was killed as he filmed the scene. A young photographer from the *San Francisco Examiner* was slain in a hail of bullets.

To add to the horror, one of the Jonestown 'defectors' suddenly pulled a gun from his shirt and began pumping bullets at the pilot. It was carnage.

At the settlement, the Reverend Jim Warren Jones called his loving

For centuries, European knights launched crusades in the name of God against the 'heathen' Turks occuping the Holy Land. But the murderous missionaries were out to kill rather than convert. The most bloodthirsty expedition was led by Godfrey of Bouillon, in response to pleas from Pope Urban II, who alleged Christians in the Middle East were being persecuted by the Turks. Godfrey's forces besieged the Syrian city of Antioch for seven months in 1097. When the inhabitants finally surrendered, every Turk within the walls was slaughtered. The evangelical army then marched on Jerusalem. Huge siege towers enabled the soldiers to swarm over the battlements and begin another orgy of death. Jews who sought sanctuary in their synagogue were burned alive. Historian Salomon Reinach wrote: 'It is said that 70,000 persons were put to death in less than a week to attest the superior morality of the Christian faith!'

The dead of Jonestown lie strewn around a vat of the poisoned drink

congregation around him for the last time. 'I warned you this would happen,' he told them sobbing. 'We were too good for this world. Now come with me and I will take you to a better place.'

There was some crying and praying as the elders of the People's Temple struggled from the pavilion carrying huge vats of poison laced with Kool-Aid soft drink. Gospel singing began as the mesmerized followers queued up to drink the cups of death.

The babes in arms died first, the poison squirted into their helpless mouths with syringes. Then the children, then their parents.

When Guyanese troops arrived the next day, they found the corpses of entire families with their arms locked around each other in a last loving embrace.

Jones himself lay sprawled with a bullet in his brain. The People's Temple had held its last prayer meeting.

One devotee had left behind a suicide note addressed to Jim Jones. It said: 'Dad, I can see no way out, I agree with your decision. Without you the world may not make it to Communism. I am more than tired of this wretched, merciless planet and the hell it holds for so many masses of beautiful people. Thank you for the only life I've known.'

Congressman Leo Ryan had a more fitting epitaph for Jones. Just before he died in the airstrip massacre, he was interviewed by the television crew. His last words faithfully preserved on their tape recorder, found under the pile of bodies, were: 'Jim Jones talks a lot about love, brotherhood and humanity and his faith and the power of religion. But never once did I hear him mention God.'

Chapter Four

THE NAZIS

Chronicling the rise of Adolf Hitler . . . and the eager disciples of the Fascist demagogue who graduated over two decades from thuggery to genocide.

'Kill a man and you are a murderer. Kill millions of men and you are a conqueror. Kill everyone and you are a god.'

Jean Rostard (1955)

Hitler: the Making Of A Monster

There was nothing to set the young Adolf Hitler apart from his schoolmates. He was a studious lad, his report cards showing regular columns of A grades. He was seldom absent, his stern father saw to that. If his teachers had any criticism of his work, it was that his mind tended easily to wander. He could not concentrate for long on a single subject. He was a bit of a dreamer.

In later years, a glorious legend would be carefully fabricated about young Adolf's schooldays in Austria. That he was a born leader whom his classmates followed instinctively. That, as well as extraordinary artistic gifts, he was also possessed of a formidable political understanding. And that at the age of 11, he gained an 'insight into the meaning of history'. All bunkum, of course. The true character of Adolf Hitler was subordinated to the Nazis' needs to make a myth, a superman and a master race. And buried so well that today psychiatrists can only guess at the boy's mental and emotional state.

Yet, at the turn of the century, *someone* should have had an inkling that there was something a little different about the blue-eyed, dark-haired, impish youngster with the intense gaze who sat scribbling at a desk in a drab secondary school in the Austrian town of Linz. Someone should have seen into the dark depths of his young mind when the pattern of his future – and therefore the future of the entire world – was being settled.

That very someone could have prevented the making of a monster, and he failed. That man was his father.

Alois Hitler was a customs official in the Austrian town of Braunau-am-Inn, close to the border with Bavaria. He was a stern man and the young Adolf had little affection for him. Alois had risen from the most modest background to a position of lower-middle-class respectability, adopting along the way a severe conservatism, a self-conscious caution and a strict, pedantic, pompous attitude towards his job and his family. He felt that he had a great deal to be proud of and even his long suffering colleagues had to admit that he had achieved much in life.

Alois Hitler's father had been a poor country miller who had apprenticed his son to a cobbler while still a child. Alois married young but details of his first wife are scant. His second wife, Franziska Matzelberger, bore two children before dying of consumption. He married for a third time but tragedy still dogged him.

Hitler in one of a series of photographs he had taken in 1925 to perfect his oratorical manner

Klara Hitler produced two children who died in infancy. A third child, a son, was born at Braunau at 18.30 pm on 20 April, 1889, and survived. He was given the name Adolf.

There were to be two further children. Another son, Edmund, died at the age of six, causing an early trauma in the elder brother Adolf's life. Then came a sister, Paula, who survived.

Apart from the death of his brother, there was a further detail of family history that was to plague Adolf Hitler throughout his life. It was that his father had been born out of wedlock. This resulted in the wholly erroneous claim, loudly proclaimed by political opponents in the 1930s and by the Allies during World War Two, that Adolf himself was illegitimate and that his real name was Schicklgruber. The stigma stuck despite the fact that Hitler's father's birth had subsequently been legitimized by the marriage of Hitler's grandfather to the unmarried mother, Maria Schicklgruber.

There is believed to have been conflict between Adolf Hitler and his father Alois throughout the boy's schooldays. Faithfully protective of his mother, Adolf found his father a boorish brute. There were stories of young Adolf having to support his drunken father home from late-night drinking houses and of having to watch his mother being verbally abused by her husband. There is some doubt about these tales but there is every indication that, while adopting many of his father's middle-class prejudices, Adolf nevertheless detested the man. And in return, Alois Hitler, the one man whose behaviour could have changed the boy's character, showed no interest in his dreaming son's high-flown aspirations.

Adolf was 14 when his father died and the family moved to Linz where Klara managed to keep herself and the two children on a government pension. It was here that Hitler decided that his future lay as an artist. The fact that his talent was slight did not dissuade him and in 1907, at the age of 18, he travelled to Vienna to pursue his calling.

It is here again that fact and fiction diverge. According to the Nazis' rewriting of the history books and Hitler's own romanticized version of events, Adolf struggled in poverty, living the life of a typical garret-dwelling artist while, in pavement cafés, he pursued a soul-deep search for a political philosophy that would lead him to his destiny.

What Hitler was doing in Vienna was somewhat less romantic. Having quarrelled fiercely with his mother, who wanted him to pursue his studies, the pampered Hitler persuaded her to give him a generous allowance. He then approached the Vienna Academy of Art which, after viewing his test drawings, firmly rejected his application to become a student. At his second attempt a year later, he was not even offered a test for entry. He had no greater luck at the Academy of Architecture, where he was told that he had not completed to an adequate level his studies back at Linz.

The vision of himself at this time of his life later presented by Hitler soon became even more ludicrously divorced from reality when just before Christmas 1908 his mother died. Adolf was genuinely distraught but her demise did mean that he could pursue his sojourn in the cloud-cuckoo-land he had created for himself with even greater ease. He was provided with a healthy inheritance, including the proceeds of the sale of Klara's house in Linz. On top of this, he claimed part of his mother's continued pension on the basis that he was still a full-time student – an act which was no less than fraud.

Hitler now spent his time lounging around cafés and joining in any and every discussion on politics and philosophy. There would also be visits to the opera, an occasional water-colour, the writing of a never-to-be-performed play. But most of the time his life was idle and unproductive as he used up the money that his late father had spent all his life amassing.

At this stage in his life, he still did not have a single close friend. And despite stories of an assault on an artist's model and of his contracting syphilis from a prostitute, there is no indication of an interest in women. The well-known syndrome of bullying father and cossetting mother may have produced an oedipus complex making it difficult for him to form such relationships.

What he was acquiring, however, was a fierce, fiery unremitting hatred of the Jewish people. In classic style, the self-blame that should have been brought to bear on his own failures was transferred to another 'guilty' party. The Jews were an easy target in the early years of the twentieth century as more and more of their peasant communities in Russia and eastern Europe were driven west by the pogroms being conducted against them. Hitler encountered these dispossessed people in his early, jobless days and, like others before and since, blamed the immigrant minority for taking work away from the 'more deserving' majority. Other traits that characterized his later life revealed themselves at this time . . . his inability to establish ordinary human relationships, his hatred of the establishment and his sudden, passionate, ranting outbursts. He was beginning to live in a fantasy world to evade the reality of his own failure.

In 1912 Hitler's inheritance ran out and he took a job on a building site, returning at night to a malodorous doss-house. For a few months his lifestyle really did match the accounts later given to an adoring nation. But not for long.

Adolf Hitler was later to relate how he made up his mind to live in the Fatherland, the heart of the German peoples, of whom the Austrians were no more than a provincial part. True, in 1913 he moved to Munich – but not for the reason he gave. The cross-border flit was to avoid his conscription into the

Only one member of Hitler's family survived to see his rise to power: his younger sister Paula. But there were those among his less immediate relatives with whom he remained close.

One of these was his half-sister Angela, the daughter of Adolf's father, Alois, by his second wife. In 1939 Hitler rented a country home at Berchtesgaden in the majestic Bavarian Alps and asked Angela to run it for him as housekeeper.

She agreed and moved in with her own daughter, Angelika, who was addressed by her Uncle Adolf as 'Geli'. He became deeply infatuated with her and clumsily pursued her, although – it is assumed – without his feelings being fully reciprocated. It will never be known to what degree and with what success Hitler pressed his suit . . . but Geli was to commit suicide under the pressure.

Adolf Hitler and Rudolph Hoess, outside Hitler's Bavarian retreat

Austrian Imperial Army. When the Munich police caught up with him and handed him over to the Austrian authorities, he sent a letter to Vienna pleading that he be excused military service. It was an unnecessary humiliation as he was shortly afterwards rejected on medical grounds.

In 1914, the events that led to World War One set off the slow time-bomb that exploded into World War Two. Through those first hostilities, Hitler, the 25-year-old failed artist, realized that he really could become a German hero. He decided that action, not words, would be his way.

Though still an Austrian citizen, he succeeded, through a personal petition to the Kaiser, in joining a Bavarian infantry regiment. Sent to the front, he was employed in what was considered the most dangerous job in the trenches – as a company runner, forever exposed to the machine-guns, shrapnel and sniper-fire from across no-man's-land. His valour was redoubtable and he soon gained a Mercury-like reputation as a man immune to enemy bullets. He was decorated twice, the second time with the Iron Cross, first class.

Corporal Hitler avoided bullets but he was unable to escape the greatest horror of that war, mustard gas. It was while he was recovering, half-blinded, in hospital that news of Germany's capitulation came through. Like most of the rank and file of the German army, Hitler believed the armistice to be an act of treason on the part of the politicians and blamed it on a communist and Jewish conspiracy. Still in the army, though certified disabled through gas poisoning, he returned to Munich and became card-carrying member number five of the newly formed German Workers Party. He attended meetings, became elected to its executive, quit the army and threw himself into the task of recruiting members. He changed the party's title to the National Socialist German Workers' Party – Nazis for short. He adopted the swastika armband and discovered his gift for oratory. He found he could manipulate the minds of the masses.

The machinations that led Hitler to final and supreme power are well documented. There was no steady rise to his eventual position as Führer; his political and brutal struggle was one of Machiavellian successes and sudden disappointments. During one reversal, when he was languishing in Landsberg Prison for his part in the bungled 1923 putsch to overthrow the Bavarian government, he wrote the major part of his book *Mein Kampf* (My Struggle) outlining his vision of the future of Germany. This and his other pronouncements gave a clear warning to the races that were to suffer most to avenge the insults, real or imagined, visited on the Fatherland at their hands.

It was a ranting, sometimes unreadable, diatribe against Jews, Slavs, communists, pacifists, gipsies, the mentally ill, the 'subversive' and the 'inferior'. Because of this doctrine of hate, not one life in Europe or throughout most of the world would remain unchanged. The dreaming artist who had no friends, whom no one loved, whose work was derided, who was shunned even by his own father, wrote:

'What we must fight for is to safeguard the existence and reproduction of our race and our people, the sustenance of our children and the purity of our blood, the freedom and independence of the Fatherland, so that our people may mature for the fulfilment of the mission allotted it by the Creator of the universe.'

It was a creed that was to destroy Germany, sentence eastern Europe to the Russian yoke, cause civilian suffering on a scale never before known, and leave many millions dead.

SS Bloodbath In The Ghettoes

When Hitler's evil genius dreamed up the genocide of the Jews as his 'Final Solution' for the Jewish 'problem', he could have wished for no more willing, obedient and ruthless lieutenants than Heinrich Himmler and Reinhard Heydrich. With cold-blooded relish, they became the most methodical mass murderers of all time, forever seeking 'improvements' in their machinery for massacring an entire race. And they logged their lethal efficiency with the pride of obsequious civil servants.

Himmler's big regret was having been too young to fight in World War One. The Munich schoolteacher's son, born in October 1900, idolized the veterans returning from the front and shared their conviction that their efforts had been foiled by traitors at home. Jews, Freemasons, Bolsheviks, Slavs and Poles were all scapegoats for the right-wing radicals whose para-military retribution squads flourished under the weak Weimar administration. The young Himmler was carried along with the anti-semitic tide, and saw nothing wrong in the motto that it was better to kill a few innocent people than let one guilty party escape.

He was far from the Nazi ideal of a strong blond Aryan superman. A weak stomach barred him from the traditional Bavarian drinking duels and an attack of paratyphoid in his teens had ruled out strenuous physical work. But his orderly mind and diligent clerical skills made him useful to the organizations springing up in the effort to build a new Germany. He became an invaluable administrator and an effective propagandist.

Himmler was also Hitler's most slavishly sycophantic follower. As the future Führer emerged from political infighting as the strongman of the right, Himmler praised him as the German Messiah, 'the greatest genius of all time.' But it was 1927 before Hitler rewarded 'Loyal Heinrich' with more than a mundane task. Worried that many men in his para-military *Sturmabteilung* (SA) were more loyal to their brigade leaders than to him, he set up the rival *Schutzstaffel* (SS) and made Himmler its deputy leader, with orders that his instructions were to be obeyed without question.

At first Himmler had only 280 men to command. But he was shrewd and patient. Slowly he compiled dossiers on enemies of Hitler, real or imagined, and built up his leader's trust by regularly telling him of assassination plots, actual or invented. After two years he became SS chief. But he was still bogged down in Bavaria while the action was switching to Berlin and the North. Then luck presented him the accomplice he needed to achieve his ambitions.

Reinhard Heydrich was also a teacher's son, born at Halle in the Teutoburg Forest in 1904. At the age of 18 he joined the navy. Tall, blond and handsome, he was an expert on the ski slopes and a fine fencer, and a delicate violinist who shared weekends of croquet and chamber music at the home of cultured Admiral Canaris. But at 26 he impregnated the daughter of an influential industrialist and refused to marry her, declaring that any woman who made love before wedlock was not a worthy wife. The navy gave him a dishonourable discharge for 'impropriety', but he was not jobless for long. In October 1931 Himmler appointed him to his personal staff. Heydrich's quick brain and imaginative cruelty, allied to Himmler's plodding thoroughness, produced a deadly double act that would become the most feared combination in Germany.

Hitler's election as Chancellor in January 1933 opened the door to unprecedented power for the SS. Within three months, Himmler set up the first concentration camp, at Dachau, and crammed it with Bavarian communists and other anti-Nazis. Heydrich formed the *Sicherheitsdienst* (SD), a counter-espionage corps, to tighten the net around potential opponents. Its targets included Admiral Canaris, rightly suspected by Heydrich of clandestine contact with the British as war approached. By 1934 Himmler controlled the police of almost every German state. That April he also took over the Gestapo, the secret police network founded by Göring. Heydrich was second-in-command. Two months later, the two organized their first massacre.

Hitler's distrust of the SA had been carefully nurtured by the SS chiefs. Now Himmler and Heydrich stepped up their warnings that an SA coup was imminent. As the damning revelations piled up, angry Hitler summoned SA leaders to a meeting at Bad Wiesse, Bavaria. They were marched off to jail and shot. SA supremo Ernst Röhm had been Himmler's patron 12 years earlier, arranging for him to join a para-military unit. Himmler had been his flag-bearer in the abortive Munich *putsch* of 1923. But now he had no qualms about ordering the death of his former leader. The Bad Wiesse killings were the signal for the SS to run amok throughout Germany, liquidating prominent politicians on lists meticulously prepared by Himmler and Heydrich. Hitler told the Reichstag that 79 died on the so-called 'Night of the Long Knives'. Most historians put the total of victims at over 500.

Hitler now declared the SS his executive arm, completely independent within the Nazi Party. And in May 1935, in an astonishing ruling, the Prussian High Court decreed that actions of the Gestapo could not be contested in court if the secret police were carrying out the will of the leadership. Himmler and Heydrich were now beyond all criticism except that of the Führer. The SS was the spearhead of Himmler's drive for racial purity. Applicants had to prove there had been no Jewish blood in their family since 1800. For officers the date was 1750. The SS leadership had to approve marriage between true Aryan types, who were rewarded with gifts for every child. SS men who preferred to remain single took advantage of the *Lebensborn* – a system which enabled them to father children by attractive, racially pure German girls. Most SS personnel were country peasants, for Himmler had a maniacal belief that towns were evil and controlled by Jews. 'Cowards are born in towns,' he once said. 'Heroes are born in the country.' But the job Himmler had in mind for his troops was hardly one for heroes.

In October 1938, 17,000 Polish Jews living in Germany were stripped of their citizenship by the Polish government. Days later, the SS told them that Germany did not want them either. Heydrich organised a massive round-up, and the Jews were taken by truck and train to the Polish border, and dumped in no-man's-land between the two frontiers. The 17-year-old son of one of the victims was in Paris when he heard of the savage treatment. He went to the German embassy, intent on shooting the ambassador. Instead he killed a minor envoy, and was instantly arrested.

Here was a chance Heydrich could not miss. He wrote to every German police chief warning that anti-Jewish demonstrators 'are to be expected' on the night of 9 November, and instructed the officers to inform local political organizers of the rules of the game. No German life or property was to be endangered. And 'synagogues may only be set on fire if there is no danger of fire spreading to adjoining properties.' He added: 'Houses of Jews may only be destroyed, not plundered.'

The 'spontaneous' demonstrations that followed left 35 people dead, nearly 180 synagogues destroyed and 7,500 businesses wrecked. Insurers estimated the damage at more than £3 million. *Kristallnacht* – so called for the amount of glass

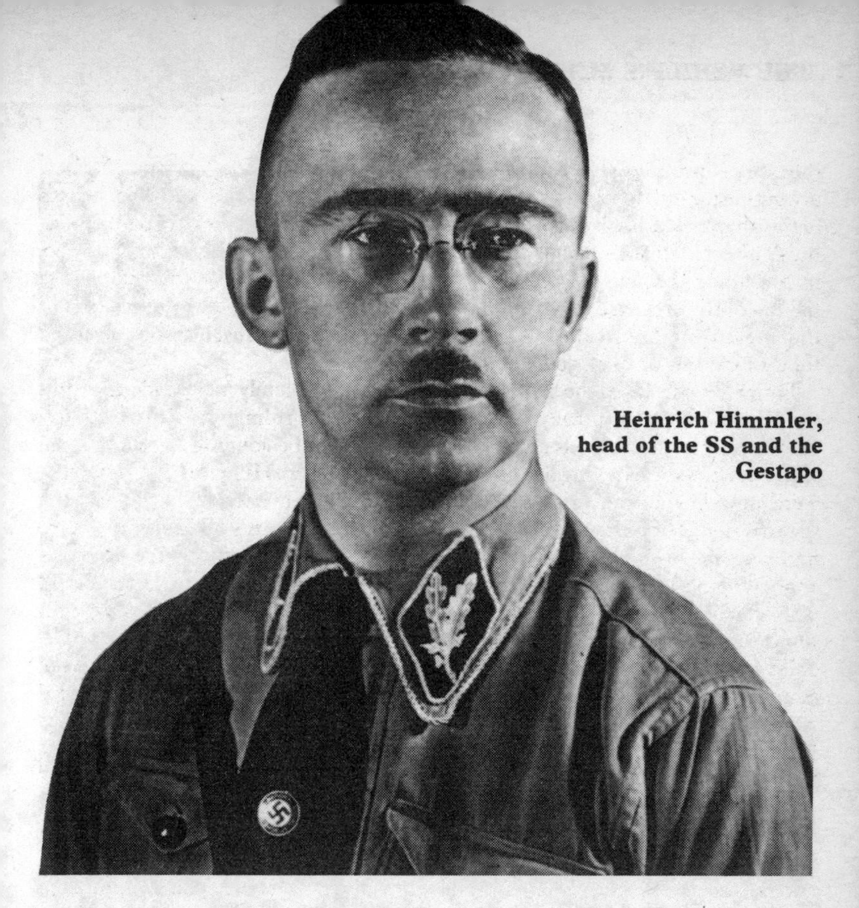

Heinrich Himmler, head of the SS and the Gestapo

smashed – was a clear warning to the Jews of Europe. Those who were able to fled to more friendly countries. Those who could not faced far worse atrocities in the near future.

Before the Nazi invasion of Poland on 1 September, 1939, Hitler warned his army generals: 'Things will happen which will not be to your taste. But you should not interfere. Restrict yourself to your military duties.' It was an order Wehrmacht officers, ingrained with a traditional sense of fair play in war, were to find hard to obey. For it was in Poland, the Baltic states and Russia that the full horror of Hitler's policies, ruthlessly implemented by Himmler and Heydrich, was to be revealed.

The SS had paved the way for war by helping Hitler purge his High Command of waverers. Many generals felt the Führer's timetable of invasions too demanding and too dangerous. Some were unwise enough to ask for postponements. Himmler and Heydrich gave Hitler rigged evidence that

Reinhard Heydrich, the 'brains' behind the concentration camps

enabled him to dismiss and replace the 'faint hearts' with men more ready to follow orders blindly. Heydrich then devised a cunning way to check on the loyalty of all Nazi leaders. He set up an exclusive Berlin brothel, Madame Kitty's, and staffed it with the most attractive call-girls in the country. But each bedroom was wired with microphones, and all careless pillow talk was taped.

Heydrich was also the brains behind one of the SS's most lucrative money-spinning schemes. After the 1938 union with Austria – the SS prepared for it by assassinating Austrian Chancellor Engelbert Dollfuss – an Office of Jewish Emigration opened in Vienna. For extortionate sums, Jews could buy exit visas rather than risk death or incarceration in concentration camps. By the end of 1939, 60 per cent of Austrian Jews had sold everything to the SS and fled. A second Office in Prague after the occupation of Czechoslovakia proved equally profitable.

And it was Heydrich who came up with the propaganda ploy to 'justify' invasion of Poland. On the evening of 31 August, a German radio station in the border town of Gleiwitz was attacked by Polish soldiers. They soon withdrew, leaving the area strewn with Polish and German bodies. Next day, as Nazi tanks rolled into Poland, German newspapers justified the move as retaliation for provocation. But the Polish soldiers had been SS men in disguise. And the corpses were inmates from concentration camps, dumped from trucks during the charade.

Within days of the invasion, the Wehrmacht knew that Hitler's warnings had been no joke. SS men were discovered shooting 50 Jews in a synagogue and arrested. Himmler instantly ordered their release. The generals had been told men, women and children would be killed without mercy. At the time it seemed impossible. Now it appeared all too probable. They pleaded for the slaughter to be delayed until the army withdrew once conquest was complete. They feared the world would blame them for any atrocities. But Himmler and Heydrich refused to compromise on the Führer's orders. They began herding Jews behind the high walls and barbed wire of 55 city ghettoes. And Himmler started his duties as head of the Reich's Commissariat for the Strengthening of German Nationhood.

The people of the conquered North were to be evicted to provide land for Germans to farm. In Nazi parlance, this was 'population exchange'. But the euphemism hid a multitude of sins. Himmler spoke of killing 30 million Slavs during the Russian invasion. And of the first year in Poland he said: 'We had to drag away hundreds of thousands of people. We had to have the toughness to shoot thousands of leading Poles, otherwise revenge would have been taken on us later.'

Mass murder was soon second nature to the SS. Nearly 45,000 Jews died in the Polish ghettoes in 1941 alone after Himmler reduced rations to starvation level. On the Russian front, appalled Wehrmacht officers watched units of the military Waffen-SS send hundreds of bullet-riddled bodies tumbling into blood-soaked mass graves. At the war trials in Nuremburg, one SS leader estimated that his squads liquidated 90,000 men, women and children in that way in 12 months. Ironically, the practice decreased after Himmler witnessed the machine-gunning of 100 helpless captives at Minsk. The man who condemned millions with each stroke of his pen retched at the sight. In future, he ordered, victims were to be eliminated in mobile gas coaches.

Meanwhile, Heydrich had been appointed Reich Protector for Bohemia and Moravia. Within weeks he was known as the Butcher of Prague, as the Gestapo ruthlessly destroyed Czech resistance movements. The Czech premier was condemned to death after a bogus trial. But Czechoslovakian agents were the link between London and a vital spy in the Nazi hierarchy, code-named Franta. Heydrich was getting too close to unmasking him. British intelligence chiefs and the Czech government in exile agreed that Heydrich was too dangerous to live, and parachuted two assassins into the country.

Jan Kubis and Josef Gabcik set their ambush for a hairpin bend on the road that took Heydrich from his country villa to his office in Prague's Hradcany Palace. As the SS chief's Mercedes slowed to negotiate it on 27 May, 1942, Gabcik stepped into the road and raised his sten-gun. The trigger jammed. As the car halted, Kubis threw a grenade. Heydrich leapt from the car wielding his revolver. Then he staggered and fell. After a nine-day battle for life, he died in hospital. The SS and Gestapo made 10,000 arrests. But the most brutal reprisal was on the village of Lidice. It was burned to the ground, and all 1,300 male inhabitants were shot.

Himmler was left alone to carry through Hitler's ghastly plans for German supremacy.

'Final Solution' Of The Exterminators

Street shootings, starvation in the ghettoes, gassing in rail coaches . . . this was how Jews, communists and other 'undesirables' died by the hundreds of thousands in the 1930s. But still this unprecedented genocide was not fast enough for the coldly efficient masters of the SS. So the concentration camps, established years before to house political prisoners, were turned into extermination camps. Gas chambers and cremation ovens were added. And, to meet demand, new 'purpose-built' camps were erected.

There were 16 extermination camps throughout the Reich but the busiest were in Poland, at Auschwitz and Treblinka. And their sinister efficiency was a tribute to the untiring efforts of Adolf Eichmann.

Born in the Rhineland in 1906 and brought up in Austria, Eichmann was an unemployed travelling salesman before joining the SS as a 'researcher', studying the 'evils' of Freemasonry. When Reinhard Heydrich opened the Offices Of Jewish Emigration, Eichmann found his niche. By streamlining the bureaucracy, he dealt with more applications than ever before – and thereby raked even more money into the SS coffers. He was so successful in Vienna and Prague that, when Poland was invaded, Eichmann was called to Berlin and appointed chief of the Reich Centre for Jewish Emigration.

But in August 1941 Heydrich told him that the days of milking escaping Jews was over. From now on, the policy was their total extermination.

Eichmann was put in charge of transporting Jews from all over Europe to the death camps. It was his responsibility to round them up and provide the special trains to take them to eternity. Nobody minded much if some died on the way in the over-crowded cattle trucks. Once a train returning to France from Auschwitz was found to contain the bodies of 25 children aged from two to four. Guards at the camp had not bothered to unload the tiny corpses.

Eichmann's hideous success became horrifyingly clear at the Nuremburg trials. Rudolf Hoess was commandant at Auschwitz from August 1941 to December 1943. Under cross-examination, he estimated that 2,500,000 men, women and children died in the gas chambers at that time, and a further 500,000 from starvation or disease. Jews were sent to him from Germany, Holland, France, Belgium, Hungary, Czechoslovakia and Greece as well as Poland. More than 400,000 Hungarian Jews were liquidated in the summer of 1944 alone, he said.

Then Hoess clinically drew macabre comparisons between his camp and Treblinka, which dealt mostly with inmates of the Warsaw Ghetto. 'They used monoxide gas, which I considered not particularly effective,' he said. 'I decided to use Zyklon-B, a crystallized prussic acid . . . A further improvement we introduced was that we built gas chambers which could take 2,000 people at once, while the ten chambers at Treblinka only had a capacity of 200 each.' The Zyklon-B chambers were Eichmann's brainchild, after a painstaking study of the alternatives. They speeded up the business of extermination, enabling 24,000 Jews a day to be eliminated and cremated. The air at Auschwitz was constantly full of the nauseating stench of burning bodies.

The SS exploited every aspect of genocide. Gold rings were ripped from the fingers of corpses, and gold teeth torn out. Bones were ground down for fertiliser. In 1942 all camp commandants received a stunning directive from SS economics chief Oswald Pohl: 'Human hair must be collected. Women's hair can be used in the manufacture of socks for U-boat personnel and for employees of the State railways . . . As to men's hair, it is only of use to us if it has a length of at least 20 millimetres.'

Crude medical experiments were carried out on captive 'guinea pigs' before execution. Sterilizations without anaesthetic, injections to test new drugs and bizarre tests of human resistance to pain, heat and cold were all encouraged. Some patients did not survive for the gas chambers. Yet in the midst of death, Himmler was concerned about life. He took particular interest in a herb garden just yards from the Auschwitz slaughter houses. He was anxious to help Germans revert to natural foods and remedies.

Utter disregard for human life coupled with concern for seeming trivialities seem the hallmarks of madmen. Yet the most guilty Nazis knew full well that what they were doing was evil and wrong. Eichmann, in particular, always took great care to cover his tracks. And as the Allied armies closed in on Germany, SS leaders destroyed their carefully compiled dossiers on who had died where. The world might not understand . . .

After July 1944, when Hitler survived a bomb attack by army chief Count Claus von Stauffenberg, Himmler's power was further boosted. In addition to his SS, police and Gestapo responsibilities, he was given command of the vast Reserve Army. Paranoid Hitler could no longer trust a military man with the job.

Himmler knew it was already too late to save Germany. The Allies were consolidating after their D-Day landings, and he was soon trying to save his skin by offering secret peace initiatives to them behind the Führer's back. But that did not stop his brutality. Field marshals and generals convicted of complicity in Stauffenberg's plot were hanged in agony on piano wire strung from butcher's hooks. Would-be deserters from the Reserve Army were warned to remember their families' well-being. They could see the corpses of deserters hanging from trees, with placards pinned to their chests which read: 'I left my unit without permission.'

Even after Hitler's suicide, as the Allies closed in on Berlin, Himmler believed he had a future as a German leader. Only after the Führer's successor, Grand Admiral Dönitz, dismissed him from all his posts as 'politically questionable' did he go to ground. With false papers in the name of Heinrich Hitzinger, and without his glasses and moustache, he tried to lose himself in the huge crowds of refugees and soldiers heading for home in the chaos of beaten Germany. But his civil service mentality gave him away. He joined a long queue shuffling across a narrow bridge at Meinstedt under the casual scrutiny of British soldiers – and was the only man in the line to volunteer his papers. He was instantly suspected and arrested, though not then recognized.

In prison he confessed his real identity and demanded to be taken to Field Marshal Montgomery. The request was declined. His captors had found one cyanide suicide pill in his clothing, but another was hidden in a dental cavity. As British intelligence men arrived to interrogate him, he chewed on it. On 26 May, 1945, his body was taken to the woods near Lüneburg and buried without ceremony in an unmarked grave. Only the burial detail of five knew where the second most sinister man in the Reich ended his days.

Adolf Eichmann was also arrested in May 1945 – but he was not recognised. When American soldiers stopped him, he was disguised as a Luftwaffe pilot, and the Allies were not too interested in ordinary airmen. Eichmann took advantage of the confusion to slip away and vanish.

It was 1957 before Israeli agents hunting the monster who supervised the murder of six million Jews received their first real lead to his whereabouts. The German secret service passed on a report from a former inmate of Dachau who had emigrated to Argentina after the war. A schoolmate of his daughter had been making violently anti-semitic statements. His name was Nikolaus Klement. And from the girl's description of the schoolboy's father, the man was convinced he was Eichmann.

The name Klement rang bells in Tel Aviv. Israeli agents had traced the escape routes of 30 high-ranking Nazis via Spain and Italy. One had headed for Latin America on refugee papers issued by Vatican authorities. His name was Ricardo Clementi. Now the Germans had passed on an address for the Klement family – 4261 Chacabuco Street, Olivos, Buenos Aires.

After delicate negotiations with the Argentinian government, Israeli agents were given permission to put Klement under surveillance. Long-range photographs were sent back to Tel Aviv and shown to death camp survivors, but none could positively identify the man as Eichmann, and the Israelis dared not make a move without irrefutable proof. Seizing the wrong man would make them an international laughing stock.

Adolf Eichmann at his trial in Jerusalem, 1961

Then a bunch of flowers gave the game away. Klement bought them on 21 March, 1960, as he left work at the Mercedes Benz factory in the Suarez suburb of Buenos Aires. He was still carrying them when he got off the bus outside his Olivos home. It was enough to finally convince the watchers. They knew 21 March was the Eichmanns' wedding anniversary.

Israeli intelligence chiefs gave the go-ahead for what was later described as one of the world's best-organized kidnappings. Simply killing Eichmann would not have been enough. Ace Nazi hunter Simon Wiesenthal had said, 'If you kill him, the world will never learn what he did. There must be an accounting, a record for history.' On 11 May, Klement was bundled into a car as he got off the bus and driven to a safe house. He was stripped and examined for distinguishing marks. The appendicitis scar, the scar above the left eyebrow, and the SS blood group tattooed under the left armpit all proved he was Eichmann.

He was drugged and driven to Buenos Aires airport, his captors posing as nurses and relatives. Forged papers declared him to be an Israeli car crash victim, fit enough to travel but not to be disturbed. He was waved through to an El-Al jet which had brought Israeli politicians to help celebrate the 150th anniversary of Argentina's independence. Within 24 hours the man the Jews hated most was in Tel Aviv.

His trial began on 12 December, 1961. The 15 charges included deporting and causing the deaths of millions of Jews, being party to the murder of thousands of gipsies, and being party to the murder of 91 children. Eichmann claimed that, by streamlining Jewish emigration in the early years of his SS career, he was only doing what Zionists proposed – sending Jews out of Europe to find a new homeland. He said he tried to organize Jewish settlements in Poland and even Madagascar, but was thwarted by others in the Nazi hierarchy. When told in 1941 that the Führer had ordered extermination of the Jews, 'I lost all joy in my work, all initiative, all interest.' Thereafter he simply did his duty and carried out orders.

The Israelis were scrupulous in ensuring a fair trial, and the full procedure of appeals. But at 11.53 pm on 31 May, 1962, Adolf Eichmann was hanged at Ramleh Prison, outside Tel Aviv. His defence cut no ice with a people who knew that, when Himmler tried to stop the activity of extermination camps as the end of the war loomed, Eichmann protested violently. They preferred to believe the words of Dieter Wisliceny, executed in Czechoslovakia for war crimes as one of Eichmann's lieutenants. 'He told me in 1944 that he did not care what happened if Germany lost the war,' Wisliceny said. 'He said he would leap into his grave laughing because the feeling that he had five million Jews on his conscience only filled his heart with gladness.'

Klaus Barbie, The Butcher of Lyons

Wartime occupied France was a place without sanctuary for those in fear of the Nazis. The German armies occupied the north. In the south the puppet government of Marshal Philippe Pétain did the Nazis' dirty work for them with an unseemly willingness. And everywhere the SS and the Gestapo ruled by terror.

In greatest fear were the Jews, who knew that unless their identities could be disguised they would end up in transports heading eastward to the terrible death camps like Auschwitz, Mauthausen and Ravensbruck. In the southern part of France, where arrest seemed less imminent, many persecuted families sent their children off to homes in the country, surreptitiously set up as refugees for Jewish infants.

France was dotted with such homes, and generally the local German commanders turned a blind eye to this slight lapse in the otherwise rigid pursuance of the Final Solution to eradicate the Jewish race. But one SS leader thought differently. He was Klaus Barbie, the 'Butcher of Lyons'.

Barbie discovered that a refuge for Jewish children had been established in a large drab, grey house in the centre of the village of Izieu, high in the hills close to France's border with Switzerland. Early in the morning of 6 April 1944 Barbie sent a number of trucks up the steep winding road to the village. Soldiers ordered the children and staff out of the home and into the trucks and they were driven away.

On the night of the raid on the children's home, Klaus Barbie sent a telex message to the Gestapo headquarters in Paris detailing his latest achievement. It read:

'In the early hours of this morning the Jewish children's home, Colonie Enfant, at Izieu was raided. In total 41 children aged from three to 13 were taken. Furthermore, the entire Jewish staff of 10, five of them females, were arrested. Cash and other assets were not taken. Transportation to Drancy follows tomorrow. – Barbie.'

Drancy was the 'holding camp' in a Paris suburb, from where two months later the children were transported by cattle train to the most notorious death camp of all, Auschwitz.

Not one of the children survived the gas chambers.

Today on the wall of the grey old house in Izieu there is a plaque bearing the names of all 41 children. It was put there after the war, to remind the people of the region of the blackest period in their history . . . Of the valour of the resistance fighters, of the shame of the collaborators who made the Nazis' task so easy, of the terror reign of the SS and Gestapo, and above all of the horrors perpetrated in the name of Hitler by one of his most ardent henchmen, Klaus Barbie.

Thirty-nine years after the capture of the innocents, memories of Barbie's infamy came flooding back. In February 1983 he was expelled from Bolivia and flown to France to stand trial for crimes against humanity. He was placed in a special wing of St Joseph's prison, Lyons, while prosecutors sifted through a mountain of evidence to build a damning case against him.

The files reveal a youthful fanaticism that helped build the 'perfect' Nazi. Klaus Barbie was born on 25 October 1913 at Bad Godesberg, near Bonn. He was illegitimate, though his parents later married. He joined the Hitler Youth and at 22 volunteered for the SS (*Schutzstaffell*, or Protection Squads) and he was posted to Dortmund to work in the SS's own elite security branch. There he met Regina Willms and they became engaged. Their marriage was conducted with full SS guard of honour in Berlin in 1940. Two years later, promoted to Oberstürmführer, he was sent to Lyons as head of the Gestapo in the city.

He quickly discovered that his task of 'cleansing' the region of Jews and subversives was far simpler than he had imagined. Collaborators and informers abounded, ready to turn on their own countrymen to win favour, reward and acclaim from their new masters.

Marshal Pétain's puppet government ensured that no more German troops than absolutely necessary were occupied controlling the country. Indeed, the French often enforced law and order more harshly than the Germans. They rounded up Jews for deportation even before being ordered to by the Nazis. Still more thorough in their new duties were French paramilitary units called the

Death's Head Units of the Waffen-SS fought alongside the regular German army in France – and sickened battle-hardened soldiers by their butchery. Near Bailleul in May 1940, British forces defending La Bassée canal ran up the white flag after fighting bravely though outnumbered. As they walked towards the enemy, arms above their heads, SS company commander Lieutenant Fritz Knoechlein ordered his men to mow them down. Dead and wounded were then dumped in a nearby farmyard. But one man survived, and testified when Knoechlein was brought to trial after the war.

Architect Albert Speer was Hitler's Minister for War Production from 1942 to 1944, and historians believe his success in stepping up the supply of tanks, planes and armaments delayed peace by two years. But Speer realized the folly of his slavish devotion to the Führer when he became aware of the atrocities Hitler condoned. He complained that Himmler's brutal SS killers were robbing him of 40,000 foreign workers a month in 1944, and even considered a nerve gas attack on Hitler's bunker to end the evil of the Third Reich. He was the only defendant to plead guilty at the Nuremburg war crimes trials, and served 20 years in Spandau Prison, Berlin, before release in 1966.

Milice who carried out many executions at their masters' behest.

Barbie's headquarters were in Lyons' Ecole Santé Militaire where he installed torture chambers equipped with whips, chains, spiked coshes, electric-shock boxes and welders' torches.

In an astonishing book about the Butcher of Lyons (entitled *Klaus Barbie – His Life And Career*), author John Beattie uncovered some of his horrifying practices.

Barbie installed twin baths at his headquarters, one filled with near-boiling water, the other with ice-cold water. Prisoners would be ducked in them alternately until they submitted.

Women were stripped, tied down and covered in raw meat. Then Barbie's German shepherd dogs would be set loose on them. Other tortures involved acid injections, burning by blow torch or being wired up for electric shock treatment.

Author John Beattie traced Barbie's old interpreter, Gottlieb Fuchs, who spoke of the interrogation of a young Jewish boy and girl who adamantly refused to divulge the whereabouts of the rest of their family. In a rage, Barbie picked them up one at a time and smashed their heads against the cell wall.

Fuchs revealed that on another occasion Barbie's over-abundance of zeal lost the Nazis a valuable prisoner. General de Gaulle's top resistance organizer in France, Jean Moulin, was betrayed and captured with eight comrades at a secret meeting in Lyons in June 1942. He was tortured until he passed out and was then dragged by his feet down several flights of stone stairs until his head was battered beyond recognition. He was sent to Germany for further interrogation but died of his injuries.

Barbie's greatest mistake, however, was employing Fuchs as his interpreter. He was a double agent, working for the allies and feeding information gleaned from Barbie to the Swiss secret service across the border.

Within three months of D-Day, the allies were on the outskirts of Lyons. By then, Barbie's sadistic excesses had reached extraordinary proportions. He would conduct torture sessions seated with a naked woman on his knee, getting a perverted pleasure out of his victims' agonies.

After a café popular with German officers was damaged he took revenge. Barbie ordered a Gestapo raid; five innocent young men were hauled out of the café and shot dead in the street.

He once called local gendarmes to his headquarters to clear out a cellar. They found it piled with the corpses of young men, all machine-gunned, their blood lying deep on the floor.

He took 110 men and women from Montluc prison and had them driven to the village of St Genis-Laval. There, in an upstairs room of an old fort, they were machine-gunned to death until their blood literally ran through the ceiling.

Allied troops entered Lyons on 3 September 1944, but by then Barbie had fled. The Butcher had ruled the city by fear for just 657 days. In that time he had organized the executions of more than 4,000 people, including many collaborators who could have borne witness to his crimes.

Barbie laid low at the end of the war, earning a living in Frankfurt from the black-market. He kept in close touch with other ex-SS men, whose tip-offs saved him from capture on at least one occasion. He thought his luck had run out in August 1946, however, when he was arrested by Americans and driven towards their base in the back of a Jeep. He leaped out of the vehicle which, in the ensuing confusion, crashed into a tree. Barbie was once again a free man.

Sadistic doctor Marcel Petiot cashed in on desperation in the chaos of Nazi-occupied Paris. He told rich Jews and others wishing to flee Gestapo persecution that he could smuggle them out to Spain and Cuba for a price. But when they arrived at his mansion in Rue Lesueur laden with money, jewellery, furs, gold and silver, he gave them a lethal injection, then watched through specially drilled peepholes as they died in a windowless triangular room. Once he was pulled in by the Gestapo, puzzled by the disappearance of Jews destined for the death camps. But he was freed, presumably because he convinced the Nazis he was saving them time and effort. Only after the Allies freed France was Petiot arrested. His meticulous records showed that 63 people perished in the triangular room – and that their payments made Petiot a millionaire. He died on the guillotine on 26 May 1946.

John Beattie asserts that Barbie spent a period after the war working first for British Intelligence and then the Americans, feeding them information about undercover Communist groups. He lived under the name Klaus Altmann in the Bavarian town of Augsburg until 1951 when he, his wife Regina and their two children set sail for South America from the Italian port of Genoa.

They settled in the Bolivian capital, La Paz, where Barbie became a respected businessman, owner of a saw mill and friend of politicians. He was even able to travel abroad on business trips with impunity.

The good life for Klaus Barbie ended in the 'eighties. His son died in a hang-gliding accident and his wife died of cancer. Shortly afterwards a new, more liberal president, Siles Zuazo, came to power, vowing to rid his country of Nazis.

France's constant pressure on the Bolivians to extradite the Butcher bore fruit on 4 February 1983, when Barbie was arrested and told he was to be sent abroad. He was driven to La Paz airport and put on an unmarked transport plane. Barbie was unruffled – until the crew of the plane revealed themselves as French officers. The Butcher of Lyons was on his way to jail in the city where he had imprisoned, maimed and murdered so many innocent people.

The Ones That Got Away With Murder

On 15 May, 1984, a cryptic agency dispatch was sent to newspapers. It read: 'Nazi killer Walter Rauff, blamed for the deaths of thousands of Jews in the SS gas chambers during World War Two, has died of lung cancer in South America, aged 77'.

An Israeli official who had been fighting for Rauff's extradition said: 'God has closed the case'. But there was one man who wished that he, and not God, had been given a chance of concluding the case against Walter Rauff for crimes against humanity. That man was Nazi hunter Dr Simon Wiesenthal, who believed that Rauff was responsible for the deaths of 250,000 people.

Dr Wiesenthal had long found that his unflagging crusade to bring to justice the surviving Nazi murderers was being hampered by diplomatic stalling and a protective conspiracy on the part of the fast-decreasing band of Hitler's henchmen still on the run.

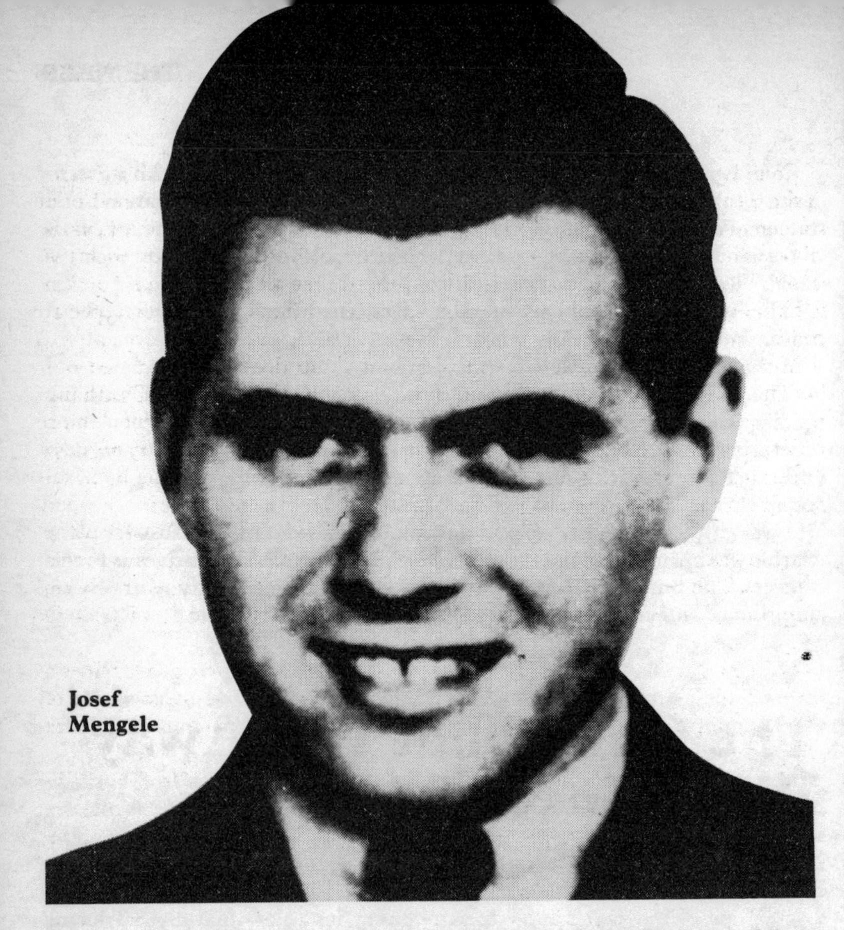

Josef Mengele

Rauff, for instance, led a charmed life after the downfall of the Nazis. Like so many of his compatriots, he escaped to South America, ending up in Chile where he ran a meat-freezing plant – quite openly under his own name. On occasions, he even answered letters sent to him by inquisitive journalists.

It was rumoured that Rauff was involved in drug-smuggling in the Punta Arenas area and that at one time he was employed by the right-wing Chilean government as an anti-communist agent.

His hatred of communists is well documented. As commander of the units which provided gas trucks for concentration camps, Rauff was known as Hitler's 'ambulance man'. He had tens of thousands of left-wingers, intellectuals, mental defectives, Jews and others regarded as 'racially undesirable' herded into what looked like Red Cross ambulances. Gas was then released into the airtight trucks until all inside were dead.

Rauff was one of ten names on a list that Dr Wiesenthal produced at the time of the extradition of Klaus Barbie in 1983. The ten names were, he said in a statement from his Jewish Documentation Centre in Vienna, those of Nazis whom he most wished to be brought to justice to fulfill his 'compact with the dead'. The 76-year-old doctor said: 'If I could get all ten, it would be an achievement. But if I could get only Josef Mengele, I think my soul would be at peace'.

Mengele was the Auschwitz concentration camp doctor who carried out horrifying experiments on humans and was given the title 'Angel of Death' by the inmates. At one time, Wiesenthal believed he had traced Dr Mengele to a remote Mennonite religious community on the border of Bolivia and Paraguay. But as a registered refugee and a Paraguayan citizen, he was thought to be immune from extradition.

Dr Mengele's qualifications for his infamous work were impeccable. He was a medical graduate of both Munich and Frankfurt universities, and it was this expertise that won him the post of chief medical officer at Auschwitz where, according to Wiesenthal, he was directly responsible for the deaths of 400,000 people.

Mengele's main preoccupation at Auschwitz was his attempt to prove Hitler's theory of the Teutonic master race. He would alter the hair and eye colouring of human 'guinea pigs' by genetic manipulation. Most of his patients died, were crippled or were blinded.

After the war, Mengele fled to Italy and then Argentina. He eventually settled in Paraguay where he became a naturalized citizen in 1973. Despite the efforts of the Nazi hunters, he continued to enjoy the effective protection of the Paraguayan government, although staying constantly on the move to avoid kidnap or assassination attempts.

In 1979 his Nazi friends in the country put about a story that the evil doctor was dead. They even released a photograph of a man on a mortuary slab, showing a scar on the right arm where his SS tattoo had been removed. However, Wiesenthal discovered that the body was not Mengele's but that of SS Captain Eduardo Roschmann who sent 80,000 Jews to their deaths in Riga concentration camp.

But neither Rauff nor Mengele were at the top of Dr Wiesenthal's list of most-wanted Nazis. That dishonour went to a man who probably never pulled the trigger on any of his victims, who seldom visited a concentration camp and who may never have witnessed an execution. Heinrich Müller, head of the Gestapo, just gave the orders.

Müller was responsible for the deaths of millions of Jews, according to Wiesenthal. Yet the inveterate Nazi hunter never came close to catching him and often had to admit that he had lost the scent of his hated adversary.

The Gestapo chief was at first thought to have died in the ruins of Berlin. But when his grave was later opened it was found to contain three skulls – none of them Müller's. He is since reported to have been in the Soviet Union, Albania, Spain and Egypt.

Four of Adolf Eichmann's closest aides were on the list. Rolf Guenther was Eichmann's deputy, Anton Burger was his field officer and Josef Schwamberger and Alois Brunner his assistants.

At his trial Eichmann accused Guenther of taking a special initiative in the death camps. Willingly accepting the task of organizing the 'Final Solution', he was sent to Denmark to rid the country of all Jews. So successful was he that he later asked to advise on similar operations in Hungary and Greece, carrying with him confidential instructions to arrange sterilization, medical experiments and the gassing of concentration camp inmates.

Guenther disappeared after the war.

Anton Burger was deputy commander of Theresienstadt concentration camp on the German-Czech border. This 'model' camp was open to neutral visitors as a propaganda exercise to dispel stories of mass extermination. But, behind the scenes, horrific experiments including poisonings, sterilization and abortions were being carried out on inmates.

Burger was arrested after the war. In 1948 he escaped from prison and was never seen again.

Eichmann's third principal aide to escape justice was Alois Brunner, responsible for the deaths of thousands of Jews in Czechoslovakia, Greece and France, where he organized the transportation of Jews to the concentration camps.

After the war Brunner fled to Syria and settled in Damascus under the name of Dr Fisher.

Eichmann's other assistant, Josef Schwamberger, was commander of the Jewish ghetto at Przemysl, Poland, where he is reckoned to have organized the extermination of 15,000 people.

The SS took terrible revenge on a French village when one of its officers was shot by the Resistance in June 1944. All 642 inhabitants of Oradour-sur-Glane, near Limoges, were rounded up. The men were herded into the village square, while the women and more than 200 children were crammed into the village church. At a signal from the SS commander, the men were mown down by machine guns. Then the church was set alight. Children who stumbled out of the inferno were thrown back. Everyone burned alive.

At the war's end, Schwamberger was hidden by the Odessa escape group, then sent to Italy and finally Argentina. In 1973 West Germany requested his extradition and he was arrested – only to be released when extradition was refused due to pressure from local Nazis.

Three other concentration camp chiefs were on Dr Wiesenthal's list . . .

Friedrich Wartzog was commander of the Polish Lemberg-Janowska camp where he ordered the deaths of 40,000 people. Some of the most damning evidence against him was given by Eichmann at his trial when he spoke of a 'spring of blood gushing from the earth' where executed Jews had been buried.

Prisoners were starved for days then, if found unfit for work, shot. Camp guards were encouraged to use prisoners for target practice, aiming only for their extremities. Only after they had suffered appalling agonies did an executioner finish them off.

Wartzog, who presided over these horrors, escaped at the war's end and has never been heard of since.

Dr Aribert Heim was director of Mauthausen concentration camp in Austria where prisoners would end up after 'death marches' from other camps like Auschwitz. Survivors said that on these marches people were so hungry that they resorted to cannibalism.

In 1941 the Germans made their first mass arrests in Holland by rounding up 400 Amsterdam Jews and sending them to Mauthausen. According to the Red Cross, only one survived. When Allied troops reached Mauthausen, they discovered the camp's log book which revealed that 35,318 prisoners had died there.

After the war Heim vanished without trace.

Perhaps the most gruesomely intriguing name on Dr Wiesenthal's list is that of Richard Gluecks, Inspector-General of all concentration camps. Less is known about him than almost any other Nazi war criminal, except that he was a Gruppenführer and was head of administration at the Reich Security Head Office which was in overall control of the death camps. Dachau, Buchenwald and Ravensbruck were under his command, as was Auschwitz where more than a million people died.

Like the others, Gluecks vanished at the end of the war.

Despite Dr Wiesenthal's efforts, chances of tracing these missing monsters became slimmer with the years. As was the case with Walter Rauff, death rather than justice is most likely to catch up with the Nazis who got away with mass murder.

Chapter Five

EVIL IS BIG BUSINESS

The cold, calculating villains of organized crime who kill and corrupt for cash.

'Love of money is the root of all evil.'
First Epistle of Paul to Timothy

The Mafia: Network of Evil

The newspapers of the time reported it in typically racy, lurid terms, as befitted the occasion . . . 'Mafia Godfather Carmine Galante was shot dead over a plate of spaghetti in New York's Knickerbocker Avenue last night. The cigar-chewing 'boss of all bosses' was sipping chianti as two black limousines drew up outside Joe and Mary's Italian restaurant. Four neatly dressed men strolled calmly from the cars into the eating house and opened fire.

'Galante, who rubbed out all gangland opposition to become America's most powerful mobster since Lucky Luciano, tried to rise from his chair but was cut down in a hail of bullets. His bodyguard Nino Copolla also died instantly. The restaurant owner and his 17-year-old son were also wounded, and the boy died later in hospital.'

A typical gangland killing of the 1930s? A regular act of savagery from the days of prohibition, bootlegging, tommy guns and Al Capone? No, that report appeared in the London *Daily Express* of 13 July, 1979 – a full 50 years after the infamous St Valentine's Day Massacre which first brought the full horrors of mobster rule to the shocked attention of the world.

In those 50 years and more, organized crime has become bigger and bigger business. But, as evidenced by the shooting of Carmine Galante, its face is just as ugly. And, as ever, this sordid sub-culture and black economy is run by the same, sinister, all-encompassing organization . . .

They may call it 'The Mob', 'The Syndicate', or 'The National Network of Organized Crime'. Older and more sentimental members call it 'Cosa Nostra' – literally, 'Our Thing'. Most people, however, know it simply as The Mafia.

Its roots are as shadowy as its present-day operations. Even the derivation of the word Mafia is unknown. It may come from a Sicilian dialect term for bravado or possibly from an Arabic word, mehia, which means boastful. All that is certain about the Mafia's origins is that it was formed in the thirteenth century as a patriotic underground movement to resist Sicily's unwelcome rulers, the French. And on Easter Monday, 1282, these freedom fighters led a bloody massacre of the foreign invaders as the bells of the capital, Palermo, rang for vespers.

A similar society, the Camorra, was founded later in Naples. Over the centuries both flourished as secret brotherhoods vowed to protect the local populace from the despotic rulers of their regions. But, almost inevitably, both abused their autocratic powers to exploit and subjugate their people rather than protect them.

America's Italian immigrants took both societies across the Atlantic with them in the last century – and it was in the city slums of the U.S. that the two groups merged. An early boost to the fledgling 'families' in exile came in 1890 when 11 immigrant Mafiosi were lynched in New Orleans. The government paid $30,000 compensation to the widows and families of the hanged men. But the money was expropriated by the criminal brotherhood.

With further massive influxes of southern Italians around the turn of the century, the Mafia took its hold on immigrant ghettoes of the major cities. At first, they were a protection agency – at a price. Then their activities spread to illegal gambling, loan sharking, prostitution and finally drugs.

The introduction of Prohibition in 1920 was probably the biggest single factor in the success story of the Mafia. The market in bootleg liquor to help America

La Cosa Nostra ....**literally translates as 'This Thing of Ours'**
Capo di Tutti Capi ....**boss of bosses, the Godfather**
consigliore ....**counsellor, a family leader's chief of staff**
caporegima ....**leader of a family's bodyguard, muscle squad or hit men**
soldier ....**rank-and-file strongarm man or hit man**
regime ....**a group of such soldiers**
going to the matresses ..**going to war with another group**
Moustache Pete..............**derisive term for old-style, trigger-happy Mafia gangster**
making his bones...........**murder carried out to prove loyalty**
omersa ....**Mafia vow of silence**
bootleg ....**illicit, as in bootleg booze – a boot being the ideal place to hide it**
hijack ....**'Hi, Jack' was the greeting when a bootleg liquor truck was being held up**
speakeasy ....**bar selling bootleg liquor – so-named because customers didn't speak of it too loudly**

drown its sorrows through the Depression was seemingly limitless. Every one of the several, fragmented, ill-organized Mafia families spread across the nation worked together to fulfil that demand . . . at enormous profits.

When Prohibition was repealed in 1933, the profits dried up and new forms of investment had to be found. Loan sharking, the numbers games, 'protection' rackets and prostitution kept the money rolling in. But new areas of exploitation were needed.

The growing drugs market was one of the most potentially lucrative and the Mafia built up French and Far Eastern Connections. Another was legal gambling, with the golden boom in casino cities like Las Vegas, Reno and more recently Atlantic City. The third was the labour movement.

Trade unions were cynically milked for the funds that could be misappropriated and, more importantly, for the 'muscle' they could lend to any extortion situation where a strike could prove costly.

Early this century, the trades unions were manipulated by New York Mafia boss Jacob 'Little Augie' Orgen, whose labour rackets earned him a huge fortune until his death at the hands of gunmen in 1927. Such Mafia notables as Albert Anastasia, Vito Genovese, Meyer Lansky and Lucky Luciano all worked for and learned from Orgen in those early days.

If Orgen's operation was the training ground for union corruption, Jimmy Hoffa's was the finishing school. No trade union has been infiltrated to a more infamous degree than the Teamsters Union. And Hoffa, the Teamsters boss, was its notorious leader.

Hoffa appointed a number of aides who had criminal records. Many were chosen for their expertise in terror and extortion. He also poured millions of dollars into his own pockets and then bought a Miami bank to look after the money. When the crusading Robert Kennedy became chairman of the Senate Rackets Committee, Hoffa became his prime and very personal target. He described Hoffa's leadership of the Teamsters as a 'conspiracy of evil.'

Because of the shady deals revealed by the committee, Hoffa was jailed in 1967, sentenced to serve 13 years for jury tampering and defrauding the union's pension fund of almost two million dollars. Four years later President Nixon issued a pardon and freed Hoffa on condition that he held no union office until 1980. That was not good enough for the still-ambitious Hoffa, who fought in the appeal court for the lifting of the ban.

Nixon's orders were not Hoffa's only problem. While in jail, he had appointed his long-time ally Frank Fitzsimmons as president of the union in his stead, on the firm understanding that he was no more than a 'caretaker' until the former boss was freed. But Fitzsimmons came to enjoy his taste of supreme power and had no intention of giving up the job. The union's Detroit headquarters became the battleground for the feud between Fitzsimmons and Hoffa.

James – 'Jimmy' – Hoffa

Although Hoffa had many allies within the union ranks, observers believed that his outlandish style no longer suited the 'respectable' image required by the shadowy figures who wanted to get their hands on the union's purse strings. Jimmy Hoffa was an embarrassment.

Shortly after midday on 30 July, 1975, Hoffa got into his bullet-proof car to drive to a mysterious luncheon meeting. An anonymous telephone caller later told the police where they could find the car. It was empty. Jimmy Hoffa was never seen again.

Hoffa's crime in Mafia eyes was that he had broken the rule of silence. The low-profile approach ordered by the families since the last war was being endangered by the loud-mouthed union boss.

The Mafia always had a vow of silence. A new recruit would hold a scrap of burning paper in his hand while he recited the oath: 'This is the way I will burn if I betray the secrets of the family'. But beyond this natural secrecy lay a more productive lesson for the Mafia chiefs – that they could operate more effectively, more profitably and with less interference from law enforcement agencies if they did not advertise their shadowy organization's existence with public killings and scandals.

Salvatore Maranzano was first to see this. The first man to claim the title Il Capo di Tutti Capi – The Boss of All Bosses – Maranzano called a conference of the major families in 1931 and proposed a constitution that would end the bitter rivalries within their ranks. But he was ahead of his time. Within five months, he and 40 of his men were murdered.

Gang warfare on such an overt scale alerted Americans to the magnitude of the crime problem in their midst. It also alerted the Mafiosi themselves to the dangers of advertising their power in blood.

The man who ordered Maranzano's killing, Meyer Lansky, learned the lesson best of all. He took up his assassinated rival's theme of cooperation. Lansky and his contemporaries, 'Lucky' Luciano and Vito Genovese, made themselves millions by adopting the low-profile approach to organized crime.

If Maranzano first voiced the new Mafia philosophy and Lansky espoused it, then Carlo Gambino perfected it. Gambino was the inspiration for the character featured as Il Capo di Tutti Capi in the novel and film *The Godfather*. Under the iron rule of this frail old man, the Mafia flourished. By 1976, when Carlo Gambino died peacefully in his bed at the age of 73, the Mafia had apparently vanished into the woodwork.

But there was just one more act necessary to make the transformation complete. And that was the removal of ambitious, brutal, old-time mafioso Carmen Galante, who saw himself as the new Godfather following Carlo Gambino's death.

Galante's life story is almost the story of the American Mafia itself. His parents

A tough, fresh 'super-cop' was called in by New York's police commissioner in 1911 and given a brief to close down the city's illegal gambling joints. The man entrusted with this task was Lieutenant Charles Becker – the most corrupt policeman on the force. Within months, Becker was running his own gambling club and taking a rake-off for 'protection' from several others.

Becker's eventual downfall was his greed. He fell out with a partner over his share in a casino and had the man gunned down outside a restaurant. The gunmen were hauled in by a police team untainted by Becker's corruption. They all implicated the lieutenant in the crime. Becker went to the electric chair in 1915.

were Sicilian immigrants who settled in the tough East Harlem district of New York. He never weighed more than 10 stone 10 lbs but his usefulness with a gun quickly won him respect among mobsters as a 'good soldier'.

On Christmas Eve 1930 he was involved in a shoot-out in which a detective and a six-year-old girl were wounded. He was jailed for 15 years but was released after 12 and returned to the Mafia brotherhood.

Galante was a man of contradictions and surprises. He made a subordinate marry his mistress of 22 years so that her children by him would be legitimate. He was responsible for destroying thousands of lives with the drugs he made available. He ordered countless killings. Yet he loved kittens and was a keen gardener. He controlled prostitutes and a pornography empire but was furious if he heard a man use bad language in the presence of a woman.

Galante's specialized business interests were drug peddling to teenagers, organized prostitution, loan sharking and crooked gambling. He was instrumental in setting up the 'French Connection' to flood the East Coast of the USA with hard drugs from Marseilles.

He had always lived by the gun and it was this loud, loutish and overtly brutal approach that brought about his premature demise at the age of 69.

Believing that no one would dare stand in his way after the death of Carlo Gambino in 1976, Galante began to encroach on the territories of other Mafia families. He was thought to be trying to amass a $50 million personal fortune to pass on to his relatives. To this end, he risked warfare with other families and put his own gang at risk from the police and the FBI.

In January 1979 he was told to give up his leadership but he refused. The decision meant that he had signed his own death warrant.

That was why Galante's assassins, carrying scatter-guns and wearing ski masks, visited Joe and Mary's restaurant on 'unlucky' 13 July 1979 and killed him so quickly that his trademark cigar was still clenched at a jaunty angle in his mouth as he hit the floor. Then a .45 bullet was calmly fired into his left eye – a traditional Mafia calling card.

Less than a mile away from the bloody scene, when the news was brought that Galante was dead, 20 ruthless Mafia bosses raised their glasses in a macabre toast. They had gathered at another New York restaurant to discuss underworld strategy following the removal of their former associate.

A senior detective on the case said: 'It shows you how cold-blooded and businesslike these people are'.

The FBI first got wind of the underworld summit meeting when a Mafia chief from California flew into New York. They saw him rent a car and tailed him to a restaurant in a seedy Brooklyn side-street. To their astonishment, it was lined with gleaming black Cadillacs and Lincoln Continentals.

Among those at the meeting was Frank 'Funzi' Tieri, boss of New York's Genovese family. Galante had been pushing hard to take over the Genovese mob and police believed that Tieri, 74, had a part in the assassination. He certainly reaped the benefits . . . for he was shortly afterwards voted the new Godfather.

Tieri had done similar 'business' in the past. He had taken control of the Genovese family seven years earlier after the shooting of the former boss Tommy Eboli – a killing that police also put down to Tieri.

The style of Frank 'Funzi' Teiri was much more suited to the new image of Mafia business-men. Unlike Galante, he could keep his nose clean, his mouth shut and maintain a low profile. He had learned his trade as a lieutenant of the infamous Vito Genovese in the bloody 1950's gangster battles for control of the lucrative empire of Lucky Luciano after he was deported to Italy. But since then he had turned to the more orthodox range of Mafia rackets – with the exception of drugs, which he declined to touch.

The Mafia was called in by the CIA spy agency to assassinate Cuban leader Fidel Castro, according to a self-confessed Cosa Nostra gangster. Jimmy Fratianno claimed in 1981 that the plots suggested included poisoned cigars and a Capone-style machine-gun ambush. There was even a suggestion that he could be publicly humiliated by exposing him to powder that would make his beard fall out.

His legitimate businesses included a sportswear firm, a sales corporation and companies operating school bus services.

Shortly after coming to power, Tieri was described by New York Police Department as the biggest loan shark in the country. They said: 'He controls most of the gambling and loan sharking in the Bronx, East Harlem, Brooklyn and Queens. And he controls gambling in New Jersey, Florida, Puerto Rico, California and Las Vegas'.

Tieri's lifestyle suited the mob. He lived in a neat, three-storey house on a tree-lined street in a middle-class suburb. Every morning he would kiss his wife (her first name was, strangely, America) and leave for work wearing a conservative business suit. He would then be driven by his chauffeur one mile to the home of his mistress, Rita Perelli, from where he ran his operation.

He was said never to use the telephone and never to commit any note of his activities to paper. And he kept the loyalty of his criminal family not by threats but by a profit-sharing scheme. The Mafia's transformation from a gang of gunfighters to a band of multi-million-dollar businessmen was complete.

By the 1980s the Mafia had infiltrated almost every area of American business life. The U.S. Justice Department named the following industries as having the biggest Mafia involvement: music, video recording, haulage, garbage collection, clothes manufacturing, commercial banking, insurance, meat supply and processing, hotel and casino operation, funeral parlours, tobacco distribution, building construction, baking, cheese making, cooking oil wholesaling and pizza retailing.

Today an American may start his life wrapped in a Mafia nappy, listen to rock music from a Mafia record company, dine out on a Mafia steak, drive a car bought on a Mafia bank loan, holiday at a Mafia hotel, buy a house in a Mafia development and finally be buried by a Mafia funeral service.

Ralph Salerno, a leading US authority on organized crime, has said: 'If New York's five Mafia families conspired to paralyse the city, they could halt every car, taxi, bus, truck, train, ship and plane. They could also shut down literally thousands of wholesale and retail businesses. And they could close down services like laundering, dry cleaning, catering, garbage collection and dozens more.

It is no exaggeration to say that in New York every morsel of food you eat at home or in a restaurant, every item of clothing you wear and every journey you make is tainted by The Mob'.

The influence of the Mafia is now so all-pervasive that more than 2,000 past and potential witnesses to Mafia crimes are being guarded by the Witness Protection Program of the US government. The bill for keeping these 'squealers' safe from Mafia hit-men is currently $20 million a year.

At one time, the Mafia was estimated to have between 3,000 and 5,000 criminals working for it across the country. Nowadays this is a small proportion of the payroll, compared with the thousands of 'front men' and perfectly honest employees who look after The Mob's business interests. A *Time* magazine survey put profits from the Mafia's 10,000-plus legitimate firms at $12 billion a year – five times as high as the profits of America's largest industrial corporation, Exxon. Add to that the Mafia's profits from crime: an estimated $48 billion.

Such fabulous rewards come mainly from extortion. Companies are forced to buy Mafia products or shut down.

The US Justice Department believes that the cost of bribing a government meat inspector in New York is as low as $25 a day. For that, he will say that kangaroo- or horse-meat is '100 per cent beef'. It is then sold, not to pet food manufacturers for whom it was intended, but to market traders and restaurants. Similarly, Mafia vegetables often seem crisper – but only because they have been treated with a chemical that can cause cancer.

The Mob controls the supply of goods to companies by its union power. Mafia men stand for election as union officials – rival candidates being discouraged with baseball bats, knives or guns. A company which resists Mafia extortion can easily have its supplies cut off by a strike or union blacking. Few can afford to resist. Most, whether they know it not, are contributing generously to the Mafia's billion-dollar profits.

Jacob Orgen and Jimmy Hoffa may be dead. But their methods are reaping fortunes of which even they never dared to dream.

The reach of the Mafia can sometimes be longer than the arm of the law. In 1984 a Mafia gang leader was incarcerated in a Spanish jail in Barcelona. Every evening, the prisoner, 34-year-old Raymond Vaccarizi, was visited by his wife, who stood in the street below his cell and called up to him. Vaccarizi would lean out of the window for a half-hour's chat.

The prison authorities knew of this innocent arrangement and allowed it to continue. Unfortunately, the Mafia also knew about it . . . and they were concerned that their colleague might begin to talk more than sweet nothings after his expected extradition to France to face murder, robbery and arms charges.

One sultry evening in July, the wife made her usual visit. Vaccarizi leaned out of the cell window – and two shots rang out from a high-powered rifle. The prisoner was hit in the heart and the face. He was dead before he hit the cell floor.

Meyer Lansky, 'Lucky' Luciano and Victor Genovese: The First Mob Magnates and Founders of Murder Incorporated

Meyer Lansky, born Maier Suchowjansky, was a respectable 16-year-old Polish immigrant who had settled with his family in New York and taken a job as an engineering apprentice. One day he passed a doorway on the city's lower East Side and saw a girl being assaulted. Lansky rushed to her rescue, fists flying.

In the ensuing fight, police were called and all three men were arrested and kept in prison 48 hours for brawling. They were 48 hours that changed Meyer Lansky's life.

The girl's two attackers were young thugs named Salvatore Lucania and Benjamin Siegel . . . who later preferred to be known as 'Lucky' Luciano and 'Bugsy' Siegel. Despite his attack on them, they took Lansky under their wings and Luciano, in particular, tutored him in a life of crime.

Luciano was five years older than Lansky. A Sicilian immigrant, he had been in and out of trouble ever since his arrival in New York at the age of ten. He was first arrested within hours of disembarking from his migrant ship – for stealing fruit from a handcart. His life of petty crime led him to jail for the first time in 1915 for drug peddling, and shortly after his release he met and teamed up with Meyer Lansky.

Luciano was at first Lansky's mentor and later his associate. They controlled a number of New York gangs, mainly Italian and Irish, involved in robbing homes, shops and warehouses.

But there was an area of crime in which Luciano specialized and which Lansky abhorred – prostitution. The Jew would have no part in the vice trade because, when a teenager, he had fallen desperately in love with a young prostitute – then found her one night in an alley with her throat cut, probably by her pimp.

Between 1918 and 1932 Lansky was arrested seven times on charges ranging from disorderly conduct to murder. But he had to be released on every one because of lack of witnesses.

Luciano was more successful in keeping out of police custody. He and Lansky had both become members of the gang of Jacob 'Little Augie' Orgen, who made a fortune from union and organized labour rackets. While Lansky concentrated on less violent crimes, Luciano became New York's most feared hit-man, whose favoured weapon was an ice pick. His reward was a string of Manhattan brothels which, by the mid-Twenties, were estimated to be earning him more than $1 million a year.

In 1920 came the ill-judged turn of events that was to turn Luciano, Lansky and others into multi-millionaires . . . Prohibition.

The soft-spoken Lansky paved the way for a new breed of tommy-gun wielding thugs to take over the illegal liquor business in the north and ensure the supply of whiskey to New York. Principal among these was Alfonso 'Al' Capone, who was fiercely loyal to Lanksy and Luciano.

In 1927, Luciano and Lansky were joined by a third ruthless killer and future crime czar, Vito Genovese. Born in Naples in 1897, Genovese had been a friend and neighbour of Luciano since the former's arrival in New York at the age of 16. A petty thief with only one arrest, for carrying a revolver, he too had graduated to organized crime while working 'under contract' to Jacob Orgen.

Despite the combined reputations of Lansky, Luciano and Genovese, the gang of three were still not the most powerful mobsters in New York. That accolade was being fought for between two old-style Mafia leaders, Salvatore Maranzano and Giuseppe Masseria, bitter rivals whose territorial battles had left as many as 60 of their 'soldiers' shot dead in a single year.

Both gang bosses tried to woo Luciano, Lansky and Genovese to their side, probably fearful of the trio's growing power. They refused. By way of persuasion, Maranzano lured Luciano to an empty garage where a dozen masked men lay in wait. Maranzano had him strung up by his thumbs from the rafters and punched and kicked until he lost consciousness. Luciano was repeatedly revived so that the torture could continue anew. Finally, Maranzano slashed him across the face with a knife. The wound required 55 stitches.

Not surprisingly, Luciano told his tormentor that he had changed his mind and was now happy to join the Maranzano mob. He was offered the Number Two job if he would first wipe out the Mafia rival, Masseria.

Luciano invited Masseria for a meal, pretending that he was now keen to join forces with him. They sealed the deal and toasted one another across the table at Scarpato's Restaurant, Coney Island. But when Luciano retired to the lavatory,

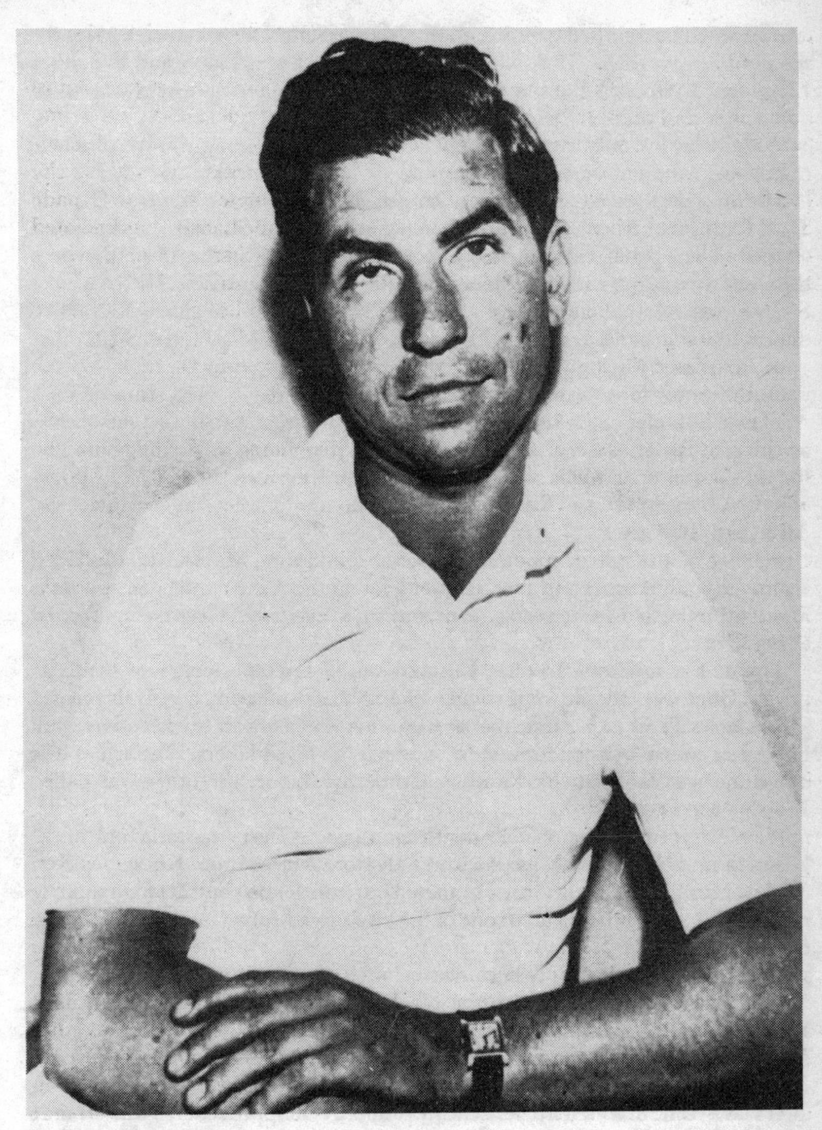

'Lucky' Luciano

four gunmen burst into the dining-room. Masseria must have known his fate the moment he saw them. They were Vito Genovese, Bugsy Siegel and two other Lansky men, Albert Anastasia and Joe Adonis. Masseria tried to flee but was cut down in a hail of 20 bullets.

Which now left only Maranzano between the Lansky gang and the pinnacle of power in the U.S. underworld.

Maranzano, aged 63, could have claimed to have been the first true Capo di Tutti Capi. After Masseria's death, this elegantly dressed Sicilian, who had once trained to be a priest, called a meeting of the New York families in a hall where the walls were hung with crucifixes and other religious emblems. He drew up a constitution of what he termed La Cosa Nostra and proclaimed himself its effective Godfather. Lansky and his associates had other ideas and in September 1931 he helped Luciano settle his old score with Maranzano.

One morning four 'taxmen' called at Maranzano's real estate agency on Park Avenue. His bodyguards kept their guns hidden as the four identified themselves as Internal Revenue Service investigators and demanded to see the books and the boss. Ushered in to his private office, the four revealed themselves as Bugsy Siegel, Albert Anastasia, Red Levine and Thomas 'Three Fingers' Lucchese. All four drew knives.

Just five months after pronouncing himself Godfather, Maranzano was killed – stabbed several times and then shot for good measure. Over the next few days about 40 more of Maranzano's team and their associates were systematically eliminated.

The mob magnates – Lansky, Luciano and Genovese – were now firmly in power. Gone were the old-style trigger-happy Mafioso leaders derisively termed 'Moustache Petes'. In came the accountants and corporate executives, still backed of course by the ultimate persuaders, the hired killers. One arm of the operation was labelled the National Crime Syndicate, the other was called Murder Incorporated.

Helping set up this mercenary death squad was Albert Anastasia, one of the killers of both Giuseppe Masseria and Salvatore Maranzano. Known as New York's 'Lord High Executioner', he meted out murder on contract for a quarter of a century, becoming head of one of the city's five Mafia clans, the Mangano family.

His growing power finally became too much of a threat to his principal New York rivals, including Genovese, two of whose henchmen followed Anastasia to his barber's shop one morning in 1957. As a warm towel was draped over his face, he did not see the two gunmen position themselves behind the barber's chair. Then they calmly blew his head off.

It was a scene of which Meyer Lansky probably disapproved. He was the man who, more than any other, welded previously fiery-tempered Mafia families scattered around the nation into a 'federal' unit. Autonomous in their own area, they nevertheless came together to seek agreement on major policy issues. Above all, they maintained a low profile; the days of street warfare were over for good.

In their book *Meyer Lansky: Mogul of The Mob*, authors Dennis Elsenburg, Uri Dan and Ell Landau quote their subject as saying: 'Crime moved out of the small ghettoes and became nationwide.'

An associate, Joseph Doc Stacher, says of Lansky and Luciano: 'They were an unbeatable team. If they had become President and Vice-President of the United States, they would have run the place far better than the idiot politicians'.

Lansky was certainly a wily politician within the crime syndicate. Despite being a Jew in a predominantly Italian society, he became trusted as an 'independent' Mafia mogul, more concerned with money-making than internal power struggles. His value to his associates was his ability secretly to invest the mob's ill-gotten gains in respectable industries and in the gambling casinos of Las Vegas, Cuba and the Bahamas.

Lansky made millions for the Mafia and an estimated personal fortune of $300 million. Seemingly safe from criminal charges, his main concern in his old age was the taxman. He even left the United States on one occasion – to live in an hotel he owned in Israel, much to the displeasure of the Israeli government. But he returned to America to spend his last years in the land that had made his organization fabulously rich. As he himself described it: 'We're bigger than U.S. Steel.'

Like Lansky, his old friend Vito Genovese also seemed to lead a charmed life. Before World War Two he salted an estimated $2 million into secret Swiss bank accounts and fled to Naples. A vociferous supporter of Mussolini (he contributed generously to fascist funds), he switched sides hurriedly when the tide of war changed and offered his services to the occupying American forces.

Genovese pinpointed black-market operations in post-war Italy and helped close them down. He then resurrected them with one of his own 'front men' in charge. His Italian Connection came to an end when he was extradited back to the U.S. to face an old murder charge. It failed to stick after the principal witness was shot dead, and Genovese returned to his New York stamping ground.

His former lieutenant, Albert Anastasia, having been eliminated along with other rivals, Genovese savoured the fruits of power for only a year before being jailed in 1959 for drug smuggling. He had served ten years of a 15-year sentence when he was found dead from a heart attack.

The third of the triumvirate, 'Lucky' Luciano, did not always live up to his name. He must have thought his luck had finally run out when he was sent to jail to serve a 30- to 50-year sentence for 90 vice offences. Then, in November 1942, he got a visit from his old friend Lansky.

'Lucky' Luciano – dead of a heart attack

All the pomp of an Italian funeral for Luciano

Lansky told him that he had just done a deal with U.S. naval intelligence who were concerned that information about Allied convoys was being leaked by pro-Mussolini Italian immigrants working on the New York waterfront. The fears seemed to have been confirmed by the burning of the French liner *Normandie* at its moorings in New York. So many fires had broken out at the same time that the U.S. Navy, which was due to use the ship to carry troops and supplies to Europe, was certain Italian saboteurs were to blame.

The deal Lansky had struck was that the Mafia, under Luciano's direction from his prison cell, would work in conjunction with a special unit of naval intelligence to flush out Italian spies and saboteurs. In return, Luciano would win his freedom after the war. He readily agreed.

At least one other Mafia man was immediately freed from jail at Luciano's request. He was Johnny 'Cockeye' Dunn who was responsible for the no-questions-asked removal of two suspected German spies. Apart from keeping peace on the waterfront, the team was also credited with pinpointing an enemy submarine off Long Island. Four German spies were captured as they came ashore from it and, under interrogation, revealed a North American network of Nazi agents.

Before the Allies invaded Sicily, Luciano sent word to local Mafia leaders that all help should be given to the Americans. Four Italian-speaking U.S. naval intelligence officers joined up with the Sicilian Mafia and successfully raided German and Italian bases for secret defence blueprints. Later, in Rome, the Mafia foiled an assassination attempt against Britain's General Sir Harold Alexander and, as a footnote to history, seized Mussolini's entire personal archives.

The American authorities kept their part of the bargain and, in 1945, within a few months of the war in Europe ending, Luciano was freed from jail but was told he was to be deported to Italy.

His comrade in crime, Lansky, was there to bid him farewell – after first giving him $500,000 to help him start his new life. He lived in Rome for a while but grew restless for the 'big time' and shortly afterwards turned up in Cuba. Luciano issued an invitation to leaders of U.S. organized crime to meet him in Havana. But before his empire-building in exile could begin, U.S. pressure on Cuba's President Batista forced his dispatch back to Italy.

On 26 January 1962, Luciano went to Naples airport to await the arrival of an American producer who was considering filming the Mafia chief's life. But Luciano's luck had at last run out. He dropped dead of a heart-attack in the airport lounge.

Extraordinarily, after a lifetime of corruption, torture and violent death, America's three moguls of organized crime – Meyer Lansky, Vito Genovese and 'Lucky' Luciano – all died of natural causes.

Al Capone and the Chicago Mob

Al Capone, 'Legs' Diamond, 'Machine Gun' McGurn, 'Bugs' Morgan, 'Dutch' Schultz . . . they are names that have gone down in America's violent folklore. In books, films and TV series, they have been dramatized, often glamorized and sometimes turned into heroes.

But the stark truth about these gangsters of the Twenties is far from glamorous. They lived tawdry lives and, in the main, died violently. A principal exception to that rule was the most infamous gangster of the age, Al Capone himself. He died peacefully but deranged, from syphilis.

Alphonse Capone, born in New York in 1899, was one of nine children of Italian immigrants. A street-fighting thug, he gained his lifelong nickname, Scarface, while working as a bouncer for a Brooklyn brothel.

This small-time hoodlum could have faded into criminal obscurity but for a strange quirk of fate. Capone urgently needed to get out of New York where he was wanted for questioning over the death of a policeman. He contacted Chicago gangster Johnny Torrio, who remembered the young thug from his own street-fighting days in New York and immediately invited him to join his team.

Capone arrived in Chicago in 1919 to find Torrio working for old-time mafioso tycoon 'Diamond' Jim Colosimo. This strange character, so called because of his penchant for jewellery, ran just about every brothel in the city, as well as various labour rackets. Torrio, a cousin of Colosimo's wife, was his principal lieutenant, sworn to guard his boss with his life. It was no informal oath of allegiance: Torrio, like the rest of Colosimo's hired army, had to swear fidelity to their leader on his family Bible.

Colosimo, with his second wife, singer Dale Winter, held court nightly at his restaurant on South Wabash Avenue, surrounded by unsavoury 'heavies' as well as by politicians and entertainers. With the introduction of Prohibition, Torrio tried to persuade Colosimo to expand his business to take advantage of the new market in illicit liquor. The older man refused.

On 11 May 1920 Torrio asked Colosimo if he would be at his restaurant at a particular time to sign for a delivery of whiskey. As Colosimo waited in the empty restaurant, Al Capone stepped out of a phone booth and, acting on Torrio's orders, shot Colosimo dead then took his wallet to make the killing look like a robbery. An hour later he was back at Torrio's side ready to shed tears and swear vengeance upon receiving the news of their boss's death. Torrio and Capone took over the Colosimo crime empire, added bootleg liquor to it and began to amass a fortune.

In the early Twenties, Chicago's underworld was split between the Torrio-Capone mafia axis and the mainly Irish gang of Charles Dion 'Deanie' O'Bannion.

O'Bannion was perhaps the most remarkable of all the hoodlums of his day. Angelically baby-faced, an ex-choirboy once destined for the priesthood, O'Bannion fell into crime almost by accident. He worked for William Randolph Hearst's newspaper the *Herald Examiner* while moonlighting at night as a singing waiter in a club which was the haunt of criminals. It was these villains who introduced O'Bannion to the richer pickings on the wrong side of the law.

'Deanie' O'Bannion was a criminal with a great sense of humour and a considerable style. Unlike his Italian rivals in neighbouring parts of Chicago, the Irishman would not allow brothels in his area, refused to sell any but the finest liquor from his chain of breweries and distilleries and ran his business from the grandest flower shop in Chicago, catering for the city's high society weddings and funerals.

O'Bannion laughed at the crudities of the Italian overlords. But in 1924 he cracked his most costly joke at their expense – he sold Johnny Torrio a half-share in a brewery for half a million dollars. He did not tell Torrio that he had received a tip-off that the brewery was about to be raided. The police swoop left O'Bannion in the clear. But Torrio, who had been meticulous in his efforts to avoid any police record, was booked. Furious, he sought instant revenge.

On 10 November 1924 three men called at O'Bannion's flower shop to buy a wreath. The baby-faced proprietor did not realize who the wreath was for. The men, Alberto Anselmi, John Scalise and Frank Yale, were killers hired by Torrio and Capone. Yale held O'Bannion down while the others shot him dead.

O'Bannion's funeral was the grandest Chicago had seen. The rich and the famous mingled with murderers, thieves and bootleggers to pay their respects to the supplier of the best booze in town. 'Deanie' would have been proud of the floral tributes. The wreaths alone were worth $50,000.

O'Bannion's funeral was the first of many over the next few years. Torrio and Capone had started a gangland war that they could not finish. Before the Twenties were out, more than 1,000 bodies were to end up on the streets of Chicago in a string of bloody reprisal raids. And the first raid was against Torrio himself.

O'Bannion's loyal henchmen, Hymie Weiss and George 'Bugs' Moran, ambushed Torrio as he left home. They gunned him down and left him for dead. But he survived, was himself arrested over the illicit brewery raid and was jailed for nine months.

The following year, shaken by events in Chicago and doubtless concerned that Capone's own ambitions may not have included him in future plans, Torrio 'retired' at the age of 43. Pursued first out of Chicago and then Florida with Weiss and Moran on his tail, he settled in Naples until he felt safe enough to return to New York in 1928. He worked behind the scenes for Meyer Lansky until 1939 when he was jailed for two years for non-payment of taxes. He died of a heart attack in 1967.

Torrio's flight from Chicago in 1925 meant that Capone was now lord of the richest territory in the underworld. Torrio had taken with him a 'golden handshake' estimated at more than $50 million but that still left a thriving empire in prostitution, bootlegging, gambling and extortion which Capone ran in a grandiose manner.

But Capone's showmanship almost cost him his life. He controlled his $5 million-a-year business from the Hawthorn Hotel in the wholly corrupt Chicago suburb of Cicero. In September 1926, 'Bugs' Moran and Hymie Weiss, having failed to settle their score with Johnny Torrio, attempted to wipe out his successor. They drove in a motorcade past the Hawthorn Hotel and sprayed it with hundreds of rounds of submachine-gun fire.

Astonishingly, Capone was unhurt. But his pride was ruffled. He had Weiss gunned down in the street at the first opportunity. Moran, however, proved more elusive. Capone had to wait another two years to attempt revenge on him in the infamous St Valentine's Day Massacre.

But first there were other items of business Al Capone had to clear up. The Genna family, a gang led by four Sicilian brothers, were Capone's main suppliers of rot-gut whiskey and gin. The liquor was cheap, foul and dangerous. Produced at 40 cents a gallon, it was sold to Capone at two dollars and passed on to drinking dens at six dollars. Many of the customers who drank it were blinded and some even died.

Capone fell out with the influential Gennas, not over the quality of their whiskey but because they were vying with him for power and influence among the Italian criminal fraternity. One by one, the Gennas and their gang were gunned down until the remaining members of the family fled, some to Sicily, some to other parts of the United States.

Another victim of this war was a crook-turned-politician called Joseph Esposito. Nicknamed 'Diamond Joe' because of the $50,000 worth of gems studded into his belt, Esposito was Committeeman for Chicago's notorious 19th Ward where he controlled police, politicians and union leaders – as well as running a string of distilleries for Capone. Caught up in the Capone-Genna war, he was gunned down in the street by unknown assailants in 1928.

Another supplier of bootleg liquor to Capone was policeman's son Roger Touhy. Capone wanted him out of the way so that he could take over his

Al Capone, the head of the Chicago mob

business. First he kidnapped Touhy's partner Matt Kilb, held him to ransom and, when Touhy paid the $50,000 asked, shot him anyway. When Touhy still held out against Capone's demands, he was framed for a kidnapping and sentenced to 199 years imprisonment. He served nine years before escaping and proving his innocence. Within days of finally winning his freedom, he was shot dead in a Chicago street.

Capone's blood-letting stretched to New York where Frank Yale, one of the men who had been hired to assassinate Dion O'Bannion, was thought by Capone to have cheated him on liquor deals. In 1927 Yale was lured to a fake appointment in Brooklyn where he was machine-gunned to death from a passing car.

But Capone's most longed-for victim was still 'Bugs' Moran, the O'Bannion aide who had tried to kill Johnny Torrio in that first round of revenge shootings back in 1924. For the task, Capone employed the most deadly hit-man of them all, 'Machine Gun' Jack McGurn.

McGurn's real name was James Vincenzo de Mora, born in Chicago's Little Italy in 1904. A professional boxer, his connection with Capone was through his father who worked in one of the Genna family's distilleries. When his father was killed by Genna lieutenants, McGurn joined Capone as a hired gunman. His reputation was fearsome. His trademark was a nickel coin pressed into the palm of the victim's hand. By 1929 at least 15 bodies had been found with McGurn's 'calling card'. His fees for such contract killings were high and allowed him to buy shares in a number of Chicago clubs. He married one of his club's showgirls. In 1927 when a comedian, Joe E. Lewis, refused to work at one of the clubs, he was beaten up by McGurn and had his vocal cords cut.

On 14 February, St Valentine's Day, 1929, Jack McGurn was ordered by Capone to rid him finally of his arch enemy Moran, who had recently been publicly bad-mouthing 'Alphonse The Beast'.

Moran's gang were expecting a liquor delivery that day at a garage at 2122 North Clark Street. Seven of Moran's men were inside the garage when three 'policemen' burst in carrying machine guns. They ordered the bootleggers to line up with their faces against a wall and mowed them down in a hail of bullets. The 'policemen' were Capone's men – one of them McGurn.

'Bugs' Moran was not among the victims, however. He turned up late for the liquor delivery and fled when he witnessed the supposed police raid.

The St Valentine's Day Massacre, as the newspapers labelled it, at last brought the measure of public outrage that forced politicians and police – even the crooked ones – to act to curb the violence on Chicago's streets. 'Machine Gun' McGurn, whose role in the slaughter was well known, was no longer wanted as a hired gun by Capone. He was simply not good news to have around.

McGurn believed he could hang up his gun and make a good enough living out of his clubs. But the Depression put paid to that. Hard-up but still flashily dressed in three-piece suit, white spats and highly polished shoes, McGurn was walking down a quiet street on 14 February 1936, seven years to the day after the St Valentine's Day massacre, when two gunmen approached and blasted him. When police arrived at the scene they found a nickel pressed into his palm and a cut-out valentine heart by his side.

McGurn's killers were never traced but it is believed that one of them was

'Bugs' Moran. O'Bannion's loyal Irish lieutenant had disappeared from public view after his men were massacred in the garage on North Clark Street. After the war he turned up again in Ohio where he was arrested for bank robbery. He died in Leavenworth Jail in 1957.

'Bugs' Moran had survived almost every other member of the Chicago gangs of the bloody Twenties. And he had outlived by ten years the most notorious of them all, Al Capone.

After forcing Moran to flee for his life following the 1929 massacre, Capone had taken over control of the entire criminal network of the city of Chicago. But his victory was short-lived . . .

In 1931, what the police failed to achieve in a decade the taxman achieved in a few weeks. On 24 October after a speedy trial, Al Capone was found guilty of tax evasion. He was fined $50,000 and ordered to pay $30,000 costs – chickenfeed to him. But he was also sentenced to a jail term of 11 years. It broke him.

When he was released in 1939, he was already sliding into insanity from sylphilis. He hid himself away on his Florida estate, shunned by his neighbours and by the new breed of Mafia leaders who wanted nothing to do with the loud-mouthed, brutish scar-faced relic of a bloody past best forgotten. Al Capone died alone in 1947.

'Bugsy' Siegel: the Hollywood Gangster

It wasn't a pretty sight when they found the bullet-riddled body of 'Bugsy' Siegel. And that wouldn't have pleased the man who had the reputation of being the Casanova of the Mafia.

Siegel was gunned down as he sat on a sofa in his girlfriend's house. A final bullet was fired into his left eye – the coup de grâce that was the Mafia's 'calling card'. Tall, good-looking, well-groomed and smartly dressed, 'Bugsy' would have abhorred such messy methods. He would have preferred a more dignified death.

Benjamin Siegel, born in Brooklyn in 1906, had always been convinced that he was headed for the big-time. But he started small – stealing cars, driving trucks of illicit liquor and guarding illegal gambling houses.

It was when, in his teens, he teamed up with the much lighter, more calculating Meyer Lansky that his fortunes changed. He called his group of small-time criminals the Bug And Meyer Gang and, by the mid-thirties, through his loyalty to Lansky, became a trusted associate of the top racketeers on America's east coast.

In 1935 Siegel was indicted in New York for shooting a rival gang member, one of 'Dutch' Schultz's men. Lansky decided his friend must leave town, so he set him up with a £500,000 investment and sent him to California to team up with local mobster Jack Dragna.

Life in the Californian sunshine was paradise to the impetuous Siegel. Soon after his arrival, he was seducing one starlet after another. A millionairess divorcée, Countess Dorothy Di Frasso, took him under her wing. She travelled with him to Italy, where they met Mussolini. Siegel and the countess launched an expedition to seek Spanish treasure on the Cocos Islands – but after blasting an island with dynamite they returned empty-handed.

In Hollywood, Siegel was on first-names terms with stars like Jean Harlow, Gary Cooper and Clark Gable. But his greatest friend was actor George Raft, famous for his film gangster roles. He and Raft went on a gambling spree on the French Riviera – until Siegel got a cable from Lansky ordering him to 'stop acting like a movie star' and get back to work.

But it was not all play for Siegel. He and Dragna operated a string of illegal Los Angeles gambling houses and offshore casino ships, as well as drug smuggling operations and even a wire service. The money rolled in throughout World War Two, and in 1945 Lansky helped organize for him a $3 million loan to build a casino hotel in Las Vegas – forerunner of the many monolithic emporia that were to make the desert town into a mobsters' Mecca.

Siegel matched $3 million of his own money with the crime syndicate's stake and started building The Flamingo, a name chosen by his girlfriend of the moment, Virginia Hill. But, during construction, large sums of money were salted away into Swiss bank accounts, some of them said to be in the name of Miss Hill.

In late 1946 many of America's leading gangsters, including Siegel's east-coast associates Lansky, 'Lucky' Luciano and Vito Genovese, met at a hotel in Havana to spend a holiday, to attend a Frank Sinatra concert and to discuss the problem of the errant 'Bugsy'. Lansky, who considered Siegel a blood-brother, argued the case for his friend. But he was over-ruled. It was decided that Siegel be asked to repay with interest all of the syndicate investment as soon as the hotel was open. If he failed, then . . .

'Bugsy' Siegel's luck was out. He opened the Flamingo Hotel on 26 December 1946 with Virginia Hill at his side. The event was a disaster. Bad weather grounded planes in Los Angeles and few of the invited famous faces turned up. The razmatazz of the grand opening fell flat, publicity was scant, interest dimmed and the punters stayed away. For two weeks Siegel struggled on. The casino alone lost more than $100,000 before he ordered it closed.

The demands for repayment of the Mob's loan became more and more insistent. But Siegel's money was largely tied up in the hotel, and the sums siphoned off to Switzerland did not add up to what the syndicate demanded. Siegel thought he could bluff his way out of the crisis, under the protection of his old friend Lansky.

Lansky, however, had reluctantly washed his hands of him. 'Lucky' Luciano, who had known 'Bugsy' even longer than Lansky, accepted the task of arranging his execution. He asked for the money one last time. Siegel refused.

On the night of 20 June 1947 Siegel was sitting on the sofa in the living room of Virginia Hill's rented house in North Linden Drive, Los Angeles, when an unknown killer or killers fired five bullets at him.

His rich and famous friends steered well clear of Benjamin 'Bugsy' Siegel once his fame had turned to notoriety. There were only five mourners at his funeral.

'Legs' Diamond and 'Dutch' Schultz: the New York Bootleggers

Jack 'Legs' Diamond and 'Dutch' Schultz were two hoodlums who brought an unwelcome taste of Chicago-style gang warfare to the heart of New York. Both thought themselves smart, stylish, wise guys. Both changed their names to glamorize their image. Both died by the gun – cold-bloodedly executed by their own kind.

Jack 'Legs' Diamond was born John Noland in 1896 in Philadelphia. Moving to New York in his teens, he followed the classic criminal pattern of street-fighting, theft and 'protection'. In the early Twenties he worked for racketeer Jacob 'Little Augie' Orgen, carrying out inter-gang killings at his behest.

The money he earned from Orgen was spent on a lavish lifestyle. Although married, he supported a string of mistresses and earned the nickname 'Legs' from a brief spell as a professional dancer. He bought shares in a number of nightclubs and eventually purchased a top nightspot of his own.

Everything had come easily to Diamond. But in 1927 'Little Augie' Orgen was assassinated and Diamond wounded. He backed out of the impending inter-gang warfare and instead set himself up in the bootlegging business. He went into partnership with an already established bootlegger calling himself 'Dutch' Schultz.

Schultz's real name was Arthur Fliegenheimer, born in New York in 1902 and following the same criminal path as 'Legs' Diamond. Perhaps they were too much alike – for as partners, Diamond and Schultz made great adversaries. They seemed incapable of keeping their bargains with one another.

When Diamond fled the scene after killing a drunk at his club, Schultz took over much of his business. Diamond retaliated by hijacking Schultz's liquor trucks.

Diamond had felt safe in his activities as long as he had the patronage of his new gangland protector, New York gaming club and brothel owner Arnold Rothstein. But just as he had lost a friend in the assassinated Orgen, so he did again in 1928 when Rothstein was found dying in a gambling club after refusing to pay a $320,000 debt due from a single poker game.

Schultz deemed it a safe time to get rid of Diamond. A hit squad dispatched to kill him found Diamond in bed with his mistress and sprayed the room with gunfire. Five bullets entered his body but he survived. Two further attempts on his life failed. But on 17 December 1931 Schultz's gangsters finally got their man.

Diamond had been celebrating his acquittal from charges that he had beaten up two rival bootleggers, and in the early hours visited a girlfriend's apartment. From there, he went home. As he lay in bed, the door was shattered from its hinges and 'Legs' Diamond was finally shot dead.

'Dutch' Schultz now had a free hand to run his liquor, gambling and protection rackets which together brought in an estimated $20 million a year. But his gun-slinging style of business was inimical to the new, rising breed of Mafia leader such as 'Lucky' Luciano, Vito Genovese and Meyer Lansky.

After a sensational tax evasion case, in which Schultz was acquitted after having the trial moved to a small and 'manageable' upstate courthouse, Luciano and his associates decided to spare the Mafia further embarrassment. On 23 October 1935 'Dutch' Schultz was dining with three friends at a Newark, New Jersey, restaurant when a man with a machine-gun entered and shot them all.

The last of New York's old-style gun-slinging gangsters was out of action for good.

Death of a President

The Mafia organization is America's 'Public Enemy Number One'. But for a long time the Mafia itself also had its own very public enemy . . . The Kennedy Clan.

The feud went back half a century to the days when, according to mobsters' stories, the Kennedy patriarch, Joseph, made a fortune from the profits of Prohibition whiskey illegally imported from Ireland to Boston.

In 1927 one of the Irish cargoes was hijacked by The Mob and 11 smugglers were killed in the shoot-out. It was, believe the Mafia, the start of a long campaign, instigated by Joseph Kennedy and continued by his children – principally John, who became President of the United States, and Robert, who became Attorney General.

Robert Kennedy was responsible for pursuing Teamsters union boss Jimmy Hoffa to jail in the U.S. Justice Department's relentless drive to crush Mafia influence within the organized labour movement. It was elder brother John who, as President, failed to give full backing to the disastrous Bay of Pigs invasion attempt of Cuba, planned by the CIA with Mafia assistance.

Many years later, after the assassination of both men, the question was being asked: was the Mafia linked with the killing of the U.S. President in 1963? At one time, such a question would have been unthinkable. But when dealing with organized crime in the USA, the unthinkable often becomes the perfectly feasible.

That was what happened in 1979 when a committee set up by the U.S. House of Representatives suggested it was likely that a contract killer was involved in the assassination that shocked the world, in Dallas, Texas, on 22 November 1963. After a $3 million investigation lasting two years, the committee's experts reported: 'An individual crime leader or a small combination of leaders might have participated in a conspiracy to assassinate President Kennedy.'

The report went on to name the 'most likely family bosses of organized crime to have participated in such a unilateral assassination plan' – Carlos Marcello of New Orleans and Santos Trafficante of Miami. Both men immediately issued the strongest denials of any involvement with Kennedy's death.

The circumstantial evidence to back a conspiracy theory was that Lee Harvey Oswald, who is presumed to have fired the shots that killed the President, had some links with underworld figures. So had Jack Ruby, the man who gunned down Oswald before the latter could be brought to court.

Oswald's connection was through his uncle, Charles Murret, and an acquaintance, David Ferrie – both of whom worked for Carlos Marcello.

Murret took Oswald under his wing when his favourite nephew moved from Dallas to New Orleans in 1963. He gave Oswald a home, a job in his book-making business and treated him like a son. The investigative committee described Murret as 'a top deputy for a top man in Carlos Marcello's gambling apparatus.' Murret died in 1964.

David Ferrie also worked for Marcello, as a pilot. He had flown him back to the U.S. after he was deported to Guatemala in 1961 by Robert Kennedy. Ferrie had also had secret connections with the CIA and had trained pilots who later took part in the Bay of Pigs invasion. Oswald's New Orleans work address in 1963 was the same as Ferrie's, and Oswald was in the same air club in which Ferrie was a pilot.

Such evidence, quoted in the House of Representatives committee's report, is circumstantial in the extreme. But judged alongside the evidence linking Oswald's executioner, Jack Ruby, to the Mafia, the conspiracy theory becomes stronger.

Club-owner Ruby's connections with underworld figures were well-established. His telephone records showed that he had been in contact with Mob

Moments before the fatal shot on 22 November, 1963 . . .

personalities in Miami, New Orleans and Chicago. He had visited Santos Trafficante. And on 21 November, the day before Kennedy's death, Ruby was seen drinking with a friend of pilot David Ferrie.

Whoever may have been pulling the strings, the evidence points to Ruby's public execution of Oswald being a certain way of keeping him quiet and preventing him naming accomplices during his trial. Ruby's own life would not have been of high account . . . he died in prison shortly afterwards of cancer.

Ruby's connection with Santos Trafficante brings the amazing web full circle.

When Meyer Lansky, 'Lucky' Luciano and their associates ran the Havana hotel and casino business under corrupt Cuban dictator Fulgencio Batista, Trafficante was a small cog in the business. Fidel Castro overthrew the Batista regime in 1959 and threw the Mob's men either into jail or out of the country. Among them was Trafficante.

The fact that Trafficante's pilot, David Ferrie, worked for the CIA may not have been known to his boss. If he did know, he might not have been concerned. He may even have approved of the connection. For the CIA, the Mafia and big business interests had all been involved in various plots to overthrow Castro and return Cuba to 'democratic' – and capitalist – rule. The CIA, with the unpublicized but tacit agreement of the U.S. government, wanted to remove the

and moments after

communist threat from the Caribbean. The Mafia and big business wanted to restore Cuba's profitable tourist industry, complete with acquiescent officials, politicians susceptible to bribes plus gambling and vice interests.

The CIA and the Mafia had previously worked together successfully, even launching joint military operations before and during the allied invasion of Sicily. A similar link-up made sound sense in the organizing of the Bay of Pigs invasion.

Even the world's richest businessman was involved. The eccentric Howard Hughes was said to have volunteered to fund one particular part of the Cuban invasion – the assassination of Fidel Castro. The plan was discussed by the CIA. Through their connections in Las Vegas, where Hughes had interests in 17 casinos, his aides recruited two Mafia hoodlums. But the invasion was a debacle, the assassination never took place – and the hoodlums died under mysterious circumstances in the 1970s.

Another sensational case in which politics and crime are sinisterly intertwined is the death of Marilyn Monroe. Again, the central characters are John and Robert Kennedy, both of whom were rumoured to have had affairs with the world's leading sex symbol. But this time the government agency suspected of being involved was not the CIA but the FBI.

J. Edgar Hoover, chief of the FBI, had long been hampered by the Kennedys in his autocratic handling of the agency's affairs. Attorney-General Robert, with his brother's White House backing, clipped the wings of the all-powerful Hoover – and earned himself an unforgiving enemy.

Hoover's agents collected every scrap of information about the private lives of every leading politician in the country. It was one of the reasons that Hoover's eccentric handling of the FBI had previously gone unchallenged. In the Kennedys' case, the FBI's personal files bulged with scandal.

Neither John nor his younger brother had been suitably secretive in their extra-marital activities. They had both known Marilyn Monroe and, in her developing state of depression and nervous disorder, it was thought that she might make public some of their indiscretions.

Such stories, which were no more than rumours at the time of Monroe's death, have since become common currency. And in 1981 a reformed criminal, Ronald 'Sonny' Gibson, wrote a book adding some startling new allegations.

In the book, *Mafia Kingpin*, Gibson said that while working for the Mob, he had been told that Marilyn had been murdered by a Mafia hit-man. J. Edgar Hoover, he said, had been furious about the actress's affairs with top politicians. So the Mafia had taken upon themselves the task of silencing her as a means of repaying favours done for them by the FBI.

Gibson is not alone in his assertion that Marilyn died not because she had swallowed an overdose of barbiturates, but because drugs had been injected into her. Even top pathologists who investigated the case have since gone into print to say the same.

Was Marilyn Monroe murdered by the Mafia? Was John F. Kennedy assassinated with the help of the Mob? The theories sound preposterous . . . Almost as preposterous an idea as that the U.S. government and the Mafia would collaboate in a Caribbean invasion. But it happened . . .

There are rich pickings for crooks along France's glittering south coast, sun-soaked playground of millionaires and 'beautiful people'. In the early 1980s police estimated that more than £70 million a year was being raked in from drugs, casino rackets, prostitution and extortion.

Chicago-style gang warfare arrived on the Riviera in 1970 when more than 100 people died in a wave of shootings which began with the jailing of crime czar 'Mimi' Guerini, 70, for his part in a gangland murder.

The spate of killings was stepped up in February 1977 after the shooting of ex-jockey Jacques 'Tomcat' Imbert. Imbert, who owed his nickname to his reputation for having nine lives, ran a nightclub in the small Riviera resort of Cassis. He was believed to have clashed with a gang who had taken over the Marseilles end of the 'French Connection' drug ring after the former boss had been jailed. Living up to his nickname, Imbert survived the shooting – though he lost an eye – spent six months in hospital and was permanently crippled.

A month after Imbert's shooting, one of his three attackers was shot dead while leaving a cemetery after visiting his son's grave. Next day the second man was killed in the street. The third man was murdered a few weeks later, shot as his car stopped at traffic lights.

The battle for power on the Riviera erupted into bloody violence again in October 1978 when nine people were gunned down in a Marseilles bar. They were riddled with 91 bullets. Five of the victims had police records, but the other four were thought to be innocent customers, shot to keep them quiet. Police, who were working closely with the FBI, said they believed the killings were 'Mafia-linked'.

The Kray Twins: the 'Mafia' of London's East End

When London gangsters, the Kray twins, were sentenced in 1969, the judge Mr Justice Melford Stevenson told them with scornful understatement: 'In my view society has earned a rest from your activities'. These activities included theft, extortion and finally murder, in a reign of terror that marred the memory of Britain's 'swinging sixties'.

The Krays held London's underworld in a mafia-like grip. In their heyday, they were feted by showbusiness personalities. They were photographed with the famous. They were generous in their support of charities. And they were feared like no other criminals. In every way, they were a British version of America's thirties gangsters, whose exploits they studied avidly and emulated slavishly.

Even after the full extent of their crimes was revealed in court and the pair were jailed for life, many people in the East End of London still spoke affectionately of the Krays. Some regarded them as 'Robin Hood' characters. Others, more realistically, saw them as people who maintained gangland peace and kept the seedy streets safe. Few at the time asked any questions as to how such a peace was being maintained and by what sort of men.

The Kray twins were born on 17 October 1933 at Hoxton in the East End. Ronnie was the elder. Reggie arrived 45 minutes later. They also had an older brother, Charles.

The boys had Jewish, Irish and Romany blood in their veins. Their father Charles, who was 25 at the time of the twins' birth, was a dealer in old clothes, silver and gold. Their mother Violet was just 21.

Just before the war, the family moved to one of the toughest, most run-down areas of Bethnal Green, shortly to become even more decrepit thanks to visits from the Luftwaffe. Ronnie and Reggie became known as the Terrible Twins because of their love of fighting – at first with fists and later with bicycle chains and flick-knives.

By the age of 16, they were carrying guns. A year later, they made their first appearance in court. They were accused of seriously beating up a 16-year-old rival but the case was dismissed for lack of evidence.

The twins were fighters in every sense. At 17, they became professional boxers. A year later they were called up for their National Service and punched the recruiting corporal on the nose. Much of their subsequent military service was spent in jails.

After their dishonourable discharge in 1954, they went into the protection business. If a bookmaker, store or club owner wanted to ensure 'no trouble', a weekly payment to Ronnie and Reggie would do the trick. As the easy money rolled in, so their gang of collectors grew. Their territory covered the East End and much of North London.

They founded their own clubs – at first in the East End, where a sports hall provided a front for their rackets, and later in fashionable Knightsbridge where the West End found the pair a rough and ready attraction.

By now, Ronnie was known as 'the Colonel', Reggie was 'the Quiet One' and their home in Vallance Road termed 'Fort Vallance.'

The Krays could be magnanimous, loyal and charming. They could also be frighteningly, unpredictably brutal. But mainly it was Ronnie who took the lead, egging his brother on to prove himself by being tough enough to follow his lead.

In 1956 Ronnie shot a man in the leg. When picked out at an identity parade, he avoided being charged by claiming he was Reggie – thus making nonsense of the evidence. Later that year Ronnie was caught and convicted. He received a three-year sentence for stabbing a man with a bayonet in a raid on a rival gang's territory.

It was at this time that Ronnie Kray's dangerous instability became apparent. He went berserk in jail. He became obsessively fearful that someone was trying to have him 'put away'. He even had to be shown his reflection in a mirror to prove he was still in one piece. Finally, he was sent from prison to a mental hospital where he was certified insane.

In true flamboyant Kray style, the family moved in to help – and Ronnie moved out. Reggie paid a visit to the mental hospital and swapped clothes with his brother. When Ronnie was safely away, Reggie owned up to his little trick.

Ronnie remained free for some weeks, during which time his sense of bravado induced him to make surprise calls on East End pubs to taunt the police. But his strange state of mind worried his family and, after a suicide attempt, they allowed the police to recapture him. After further treatment, he was deemed fit to be released, in 1958.

But Ronnie Kray was far from cured – and no one knew it better than his brother. Reggie had a good business brain, and the family's commercial enterprises had flourished during Ronnie's spell in jail. There was the original 'Double R Club' in Bow, a new club in Stratford, a car sales business and even an illegal gambling club a stone's throw away from Bow police station. But

The Kray twins, Reggie (left) and Ronnie (right), with brother Charles

Ronnie's return from prison also meant a return of the heavy-handed gangsterism that put such businesses in peril.

The brothers argued about their 'firm'. But when in 1960 Reggie was jailed for 18 months for demanding money with menaces, it was his brother's turn to have a free hand at running the business.

Ronnie took a contract from the notorious slum landlord, Peter Rachman. The Krays' hoodlums would guard Rachman's rent collectors in return for a healthy commission. The result was not only added riches for Ronnie but his introduction to a more sophisticated society. His new Knightsbridge club, 'Esmerelda's Barn', became a favourite rendezvous for entertainers and sports people. It also became a haven for penniless young men on the make . . . for Ronnie was by now openly homosexual.

Reggie was otherwise inclined. When released from prison in 1961, he fell hopelessly in love with a 16-year-old East End girl. For the first time in their lives, the brother's lifestyles were now widely different – Ronnie veered towards his swinging friends 'up West' while Reggie returned to his roots on the east side of town. Largely thanks to Reggie's business acumen, the Krays added a restaurant and several other clubs to their empire. And Reggie got married – tragically for his teenage bride who could not cope with the gangster's crazy world and eventually committed suicide in 1967.

It may have been due to the strain of Reggie's failing marriage or it may have been due to the Al Capone fantasy world of brother Ronnie, but the regime of the Krays took an even more violent turn in the second half of the Sixties.

There were beatings, brandings and knifings. One former friend who drunkenly insulted Ronnie needed 70 stitches to face wounds. There were also at least three unsuccessful attempts on the Krays' lives, and Ronnie took to sleeping with a gun under his pillow.

Warfare flared between the Krays and Charles Richardson's gang, based in south London but intent on muscling in on West End protection rackets.

In March 1966, a small-time 'heavy' working for Richardson strayed into Kray territory. The brothers were told that George Cornell had been announcing to East Enders that 'Ronnie Kray is a big, fat poof and don't take any notice of him . . . He can't protect you from anything.'

Ronnie was tipped off that Cornell was in a well-known Whitechapel pub called the Blind Beggar. Ronnie walked calmly into the bar and, as he later described in his own words, 'put a gun at his head, looked him in the eyes and pulled the trigger. Then I put the gun in my pocket. His body fell off the stool and I walked out.'

Later he justified the murder by saying: 'Cornell was vermin. He was a drunkard and a bully. He was simply nothing. I done the Earth a favour ridding it of him.'

The following year, Reggie made his own violent contribution to the murder statistics.

By now, the brothers' business had expanded to drugs and pornography, areas that did not endear them to their traditional East End friends. Ronnie's homosexual proclivities were the talk of their 'manor' – quite apart from his by-now obvious paranoia. And Reggie 'the Quiet One', following his wife's suicide, had taken to drink and to shooting at the legs of people who gave him offence.

The Krays were becoming bad news. They were being shunned by the rich and famous as well as by the poor and infamous. They were trouble. The twins became concerned about their 'image' and decided to hold a test of their 150-strong gang's loyalty – a meaningless murder.

The victim was to be Jack 'The Hat' McVitie, so called because of the hat he wore to hide his baldness. McVitie's crime was to owe the brothers £500 and to have insulted them in their absence during a drunken binge.

Four of the Krays' men lured McVitie to a 'party' in a borrowed house in Stoke Newington where Ronnie, Reggie and two henchmen lay in wait. As their victim entered he realized his impending fate and turned to flee. Ronnie pinned him against a wall and told him: 'Come on, Jack, be a man.' McVitie said: 'I will be a man but I don't want to die like one.'

Ronnie led him into a basement room where the killing became near-farcical. As McVitie walked through the door, Reggie pointed a gun at his head and pulled the trigger . . . nothing happened. Ronnie then picked up a carving knife and thrust it at McVitie's back. But it failed to pierce his thick coat.

McVitie made a dash for the window. He dived through, only to be grabbed by his feet and hauled back in. Ronnie pinioned his arms from behind and screamed at his brother: 'Kill him, Reg. Do it. Don't stop now.' Reggie picked up the knife and stabbed his pleading victim in the face and then through the throat. The knife passed through his gullet and pinned him to the floor.

McVitie's body was never found.

Flushed with their success, the twins decided to form a Murder Incorporated organization along the lines of the American model. But, by now, every move they made was being monitored by a Scotland Yard team led by Detective Superintendent Leonard 'Nipper' Read.

Plans were laid to kill a minor crook who was appearing as a witness at an Old Bailey trial. The murder weapons were a crossbow and a briefcase with a hidden hypodermic syringe filled with cyanide. Another plan was for the contract killing of a gambler who owed an unspecified debt to the Krays' prospective paymasters in Las Vegas. A third plot was to be the murder of a Maltese club owner by blowing up his car with dynamite.

Detective Superintendent 'Nipper' Read's case against the Krays was now strong. But he knew that, unless the twins were safely behind bars, prospective witnesses would suffer 'memory loss' or simply vanish.

Then the police got lucky. A Kray associate was stopped while about to board a plane from Glasgow to London. He was carrying four sticks of dynamite, presumably destined for the Maltese club-owner's car. Detectives raided his home and found the crossbow and briefcase complete with poisonous syringe.

On the night of 8 May 1968 Ronnie and Reggie went drinking at the Old Horn pub in Bethnal Green. They went on to the Astor Club in fashionable Berkeley Square, returning to their mother's new council flat in Shoreditch at four in the morning. Reggie went to bed with a girlfriend, Ronnie with a boyfriend. At dawn 'Nipper' Read's men swooped on the flat and arrested them.

The Kray twins were charged with the murders of George Cornell and Jack McVitie. Eight other members of their 'firm', including their brother Charles, were charged with various lesser crimes.

The twins pleaded not guilty but after a sensational 39-day trial at the Old Bailey, they were jailed for life with a recommendation that they should serve no less than 30 years. They were 35 years of age when the trial ended on 8 March 1969, which meant that they would be pensioners before they were released.

Ronnie and Reggie were sent to separate top-security prisons. In 1972 they were briefly reunited at Parkhurst jail on the Isle of Wight. But in 1979 Ronnie was again certified and sent to Broadmoor hospital for the criminally insane.

Reggie found his sentence harder to take than his brother. He was classified as a Category A prisoner – highly dangerous and liable to escape. Shadowed at all times by two prison officers, his movements were logged and monitored while his visits were screened and limited. While of Category A status, no parole board could consider his case. All his appeals fell on deaf ears. In 1982, he unsuccessfully attempted suicide by cutting his wrists.

Ronnie was luckier in his time behind bars. Being an inmate of Broadmoor, he was allowed more privileges than his brother. He received visits from old East End associates and from showbusiness and sporting friends. They brought him parcels of food from Harrods – smoked salmon and game pie – and classical records for the hi-fi in his cell. He also had a colour television set.

Ronnie Kray would regale visitors with details of his exploits in the days when he and his brother wrote headlines in blood. In 1983 he told a visiting journalist, long-time friend Brian Hitchen: 'We never hurt ordinary members of the public. We only took money off other villains and gave a bundle of that away to decent people who were on hard times.

'I look back on those days and naturally remember the good times. Then, people could take ladies into pubs with them without the risk of their being insulted. Old people didn't get mugged, either. It couldn't have happened when we were looking after the East End.'

About life in Broadmoor he said: 'There are some really bad ones in here,

Brian, some really bad ones. But they are all some mother's sons – and that's where the heartbreak is. Because no matter what they've done or how bad they've been, the mothers don't stop coming and don't stop loving them. When I see these mums, I feel really sorry for them having to come here.'

In 1982 the twins' strongest link with the outside world ended. Their most constant visitor, their mother Violet, died one week before her seventy-third birthday. Violet Kray had become an East End legend in her own right and was said to have been the only person on earth who had any control over the twins.

Ronnie and Reggie were allowed out for a day to attend her funeral, which was turned into a star-studded East End occasion.

Reggie said after his return to Parkhurst jail: 'It's so lonely without visits from our mum. They were always the best ones. I shall miss her so much. Throughout the funeral, Ronnie and I were handcuffed to police officers who must have been 6ft. 3ins. (1.9 metres) tall. But they needn't have worried. Violence is not part of my life anymore.

'I get angry when I read about the way things are in the East End nowadays – like those attacks on old ladies. Years ago, if we saw an old lady we would help her across the road and wish her goodnight. Now they rape 80-year-old women and kill them for their pensions. It makes me sick.'

And of the hopelessness of life in jail, he said: 'You can so easily give up after all these years. They have passed quickly. But it is only when I see the youngsters come in here that I realize what a terrible waste of life it is.'

The Richardson Gang: Scourge of South London

If the Krays were infamous for meting out instant vengeance, the rival Richardson gang, based on the south side of the Thames, were the masters of the slower punishment. They vied with the Krays for the reputation of being the most monstrous merchants of terror in London. Known as the 'torture gang', their speciality was pinning their enemies to the floor with six-inch (15 cm) nails and removing their toes with bolt cutters.

The gang's leader was Charles Richardson, born in Camberwell in 1934. He and his younger brother Eddie turned to crime after their father left home –

leaving the family without any source of income – while the children were still schoolboys.

From petty theft, the brothers slowly built up a thriving string of businesses – some legitimate, others not – throughout south London. Charles specialized in scrap metal but he also ran furniture and fancy goods firms. Eddie operated fruit machines and a wholesale chemists' supplier.

On their own, these companies would have made the brothers comfortably well off, although not rich. But largely they were no more than fronts for the other and more profitable sides of their business – fraud, theft and receiving stolen goods.

Eddie's fruit machine business, for instance, was more successful than most in the same line. The reason was simple – if a pub or club owner was offered one of Eddie's machines, he would be wise to accept. If not, he knew his premises would be broken into, and vandalized, or quite openly smashed up, by 'heavies' in broad daylight.

The Richardsons' most masterful money-making strokes, however, involved what were known as 'long firms'. A company would be set up under a Richardson nominee and begin trading perfectly legitimately. Goods would be ordered from suppliers and paid for promptly, so creating good credit ratings. After a few months' operation, massive orders would be placed on credit with all the suppliers. The goods would be quickly sold, the Richardsons would pocket the money, and the company would seemingly evaporate into thin air.

Charles was once arrested for receiving stolen goods, but police had to drop the charge for lack of evidence. They kept a careful watch on the gang's activities, however, and in 1965 they got an insight into the full horrors of the Richardsons' methods for keeping order and repaying old scores.

In July of that year one of the gang's victims walked into a South London police station and related a horrific story of how he had been tortured by the gang after a kangaroo court had found him guilty of disloyalty. Finally, he had been forced to mop up his own blood from the floor.

The trials and torture sessions were, police discovered, the sadistic speciality of Eddie. Sick with fear, the victims would be hauled in by gang members and tried before Eddie and the others in a mock court. Then the punishments were meted out – anything from beatings to more fearsome forms of torture. Men were whipped, burned with cigarettes, had their teeth pulled out with pliers, were nailed to the floor, had their toes removed by bolt cutters or leaped in agony from the effects of an electric shock machine. Afterwards if the victims were too badly injured they would be taken to a struck-off doctor for emergency treatment.

In 1966 the police decided they had enough evidence to act. The clincher was the murder trial of a man accused of killing a South African mining speculator to whom Charles Richardson was said to have entrusted a considerable sum of money which had never been returned. There were also stories about Charles being involved with the South African secret service, BOSS – and even talk of an attempt to bug the telephone of Prime Minister Harold Wilson.

Eddie was by now already inside jail, serving five years for affray. In July 1966 police mopped up the rest of the gang in a series of raids throughout south-east London.

It was not until April 1967 that the Old Bailey trial began, with charges of fraud, extortion, assaults and grievous bodily harm. Despite an attempt to bribe a juror, the Richardsons were found guilty after 46 days of evidence. Eddie had another ten years added to his existing sentence. Charles was jailed for 25 years for grievous bodily harm, demanding money with menaces and robbery with violence.

The judge, Mr Justice Lawton, told him: 'You terrorized those who crossed your path in a way that was vicious, sadistic and a disgrace to society . . . One is ashamed to think one lives in a society that contains men like you. You must be prevented from committing further crime. It must be made clear that all those who set themselves up as gang leaders will be struck down, as you have been struck down.'

Like the Kray brothers, Charles Richardson was later to issue an apologia for his crimes. He said: 'The men I was involved with were professional swindlers. I was only trying to get my own money back. I feel sick about the way I have been portrayed. I'm a scapegoat. I got 25 years for grievous bodily harm and not one of them need an aspirin.'

He told the London *Sunday Times* in 1983 that his links with South Africa and the shadowy BOSS organization had been an embarrassment to the British

Pride swelled in Jimmy Eppolito's chest as he posed for a photograph beside U.S. President Jimmy Carter's wife Rosalynn. But when Eppolito later flaunted the picture, his underworld bosses were far from amused. They sentenced him to death for 'showboating' – attracting unwanted publicity to the Mafia.

Eppolito, 34, who worked for Carlo Gambino's New York crime family as well as helping out the Carters' favourite children's charity in his spare time, was lured to a non-existent business appointment in March 1980. As he and his 64-year-old father waited in their car, they were machine-gunned to death by unknown assailants.

government. 'I was a pawn,' he said. 'The bigger a criminal the British made me out to be, the more leverage they could apply on the South Africans for having used me. Most business is pressure and blackmail, isn't it?

'I never tapped Harold Wilson's phone – it could have been done but it wasn't. But people here got very upset about that. They wanted to get rid of me for as long as possible.'

A vociferous campaign for his early release was launched by Charles Richardson's loyal family and friends, backed by parole board reports stating that he was no longer a danger to society. They fell on deaf ears.

In 1980 he walked out of an open prison and went on the run for nearly a year, supposedly to publicize his claims for freedom. He even dressed up as Father Christmas and handed out presents at a children's party. On his return to prison, he was allowed a day release to work with the handicapped. In 1983, anticipating his early release within a year or two, he was allowed home for a long, quiet weekend to prepare himself for life again on the outside.

A preview of the lifestyle befitting one of the biggest ex-crooks in London was revealed when he was collected at the gates of Coldingley Open Prison, Berkshire, by Rolls-Royce. He was driven home for a family reunion, then took his relatives – including his freed brother Eddie – to a champagne lunch.

In the following days the festivities continued at a nightclub and a public house. At the Sidmouth Arms, off the Old Kent Road in the Richardsons' old stamping ground, 350 people thronged the bars and lounges to pay their respects to Charles.

'Look around you,' he told reporters. 'I love these people and they love me. I get 200 Christmas cards a year in jail. That's what a bad man I am.'

Charles Richardson was finally freed from prison in July 1984.

Chapter Six

BLOOD LUST

More savage than any animal, these men committed the most horrifying crimes of all. Mass murderers, sex monsters, cannibals or vampires, they all enjoyed letting blood. From the insane Roman Emperor who butchered his countrymen and turned his sisters into prostitutes to the insidious writer who polluted the minds of the weak with his creed of cruelty – and gave the world the word Sadism.

'Man is the only animal who causes pain to others with no other object than wanting to do so.'

Arthur Schopenhauer (1851)

Caligula

There was relief and rejoicing in Rome in AD 37 when 25-year-old Gaius Caesar succeeded to the title of Emperor from the elderly tyrant Tiberius. Tiberius, who had spent brooding years of self-imposed exile on the island of Capri, had become feared and despised because of the cruel executions of his critics in the Roman army.

But it seemed as if the embittered old emperor might have done some sort of penance by appointing Gaius Caesar as his successor. The young man was a great-grandson of Augustus and son of the soldier Germanicus, one of the unsullied military heroes of the Roman Empire.

As a baby, Gaius had often been taken by his father on Roman army campaigns and the legionaires who doted on the child adopted him as a lucky mascot. They dressed him in a tiny uniform complete with hand-crafted boots, called caligae. And they gave him the fond nickname 'Caligula' – little boots. In four brief years that nickname was to strike terror into the hearts of the citizens of Rome and even the old soldiers who helped to rear him.

Caligula had a wild streak of youthful extravagance and an appetite for sexual adventuring. But if his elders thought he would grow out of such excesses as he adopted the mature responsibilities of Emperor, they were mistaken. His youthful excesses masked a depraved insanity which only surfaced when he began to revel in the full power of his new office.

The first six months of Caligula's reign were a spectacular 'honeymoon' period for the citizens of Rome. He quickly won their affection by giving away most of the treasury of Tiberius in generous tax rebates and cash bonuses for the soldiers of the garrison in Rome. And he paid small fortunes to the soldiers he trusted most – the broad-shouldered German mercenaries who made up his personal bodyguard.

With reckless disregard for the worried senators who warned him he would bankrupt himself and the office of Emperor, he began to lavish unheard-of expense on the blood-letting rituals of the circuses in the Roman amphitheatres.

From all parts of the Empire, a sinister menagerie of lions, panthers, elephants and bears were captured in the forests and deserts to be brought to Rome and bloodily butchered in staged 'hunts' in the arenas, to the delight of the spectators.

Prize money for gladiators and charioteers was doubled and trebled to encourage them to fight each other to the death at the circuses. The shows were breathtaking extravaganzas, wildly acclaimed by their audiences – and they made Caligula an Emperor to be admired and applauded.

The popularity of the circuses also helped his subjects turn a blind eye to the fact that Caligula had made his three sisters leave their husbands and move into his palace in Rome to share his bed. And it helped to stifle any misgivings about reports that the fun-loving young Emperor spent many nights wandering the city with his guards, indulging in orgies with the prostitutes before burning their brothels to the ground.

In AD 38, with his reign only a year old, Caligula was still a popular Emperor when he fell ill with a fever. The circuses suddenly stopped.

Sympathetic Romans gathered in their thousands day and night outside his palace. All traffic of chariots and handcarts, and the noise of music and trade in the street were banned within half a mile of the palace, while the citizens prayed for Caligula's recovery.

For a month he hovered between life and death. Then the fever broke. The Emperor awoke weakened but growing stronger every day. But he had gone stark, raving mad.

Calling his friends and family around him, he confided: 'I wasn't really ill, I was just being reborn as a God!'

And with just enough money left at his disposal, Caligula celebrated with a programme of circuses which surpassed all his previous spectaculars. He was determined that everyone should enjoy themselves as much as he did. Trade and commerce almost ground to a halt as Caligula declared day after day a public holiday so that none of the citizens might have an excuse for not attending the circuses.

The constant bloody carnival soon took its toll. For the Romans, it was too much of a good thing. And for Caligula's purse, it was an expense he could no longer support. With most of his money gone in spendthrift celebration, even the Emperor felt the pinch of the expense of fresh meat to feed the lions being prepared for their daily battle with gladiators – who were themselves deserting the circus because of the falling prize money.

And when one mediocre circus featured mangy, underfed lions and paunchy, middle-aged gladiators lured from retirement, it was unacceptable to the crowds, who demanded more and more excitement each time. They rose in the 30,000 seat amphitheatre and actually booed the Emperor.

The mad Caligula reacted swiftly. The ringleaders who had led the jeering were seized by his guards and dragged away to the cellars under the arena. There their tongues were cut out and, choking on their own blood, they were forced into the arena to do battle with the wild animals.

The Roman crowd, used to seeing trained professional 'huntsmen' kill the lions, were stunned into silence by the sight of their fellow citizens being made to

The victims who suffered most from the sexual depravity of the Emperor Caligula were members of his own family. It is likely that his own grandmother, who was besotted by him as a boy, introduced him to sex. As a 13-year-old, he began to have an incestuous affair with his sister Drusilla, who was one year older than him. When he became emperor he forced his two other sisters, Agrippinilla and Lesbia, to divorce their husbands and to share his bed with him. But it was Drusilla who paid the ultimate price. When she became pregnant, the emperor believed that she was going to give birth to his child and that the baby of their incestuous union would be endowed with God-like powers. Drusilla died in one night of bloody butchery, when Caligula disembowelled her to pluck the unborn baby from her womb. The emperor announced that his beloved sister had died of a crippling disease and her body was hastily bound in a tight shroud and buried before any mourner could see the bestial wounds and dismemberment he had inflicted on her.

face the beasts. But Caligula enjoyed the scene immensely, whooping and clapping until the last of the insolent hecklers had been killed and dragged back to the cages by the emaciated lions.

As he left the arena with a mad glint in his eye, he told the Captain of the Guard wistfully: 'I only wish all of Rome had just one neck so I could cut off all their heads with one blow.'

Caligula had cowed even the bloodthirsty Romans into shocked submission. Still he needed more money to stage even more circuses and to keep paying his army for their shaken loyalty. And mad though he was, he knew that nothing would bring the wrath of his disenchanted subjects down on him quicker than a hefty increase in their taxes.

At least he had solved the problem of the food bill for the lions. From then on, the common criminals of Rome's jails were transported to the amphitheatres at night and fed to the lions. He began to ease his other financial problems with a series of trumped-up treason charges against some of the capital's wealthiest citizens. Their vast estates and fortunes were seized as fines and punishment, and the paid informers who gave perjured evidence against them were rewarded with a few gold coins.

With all of Rome turning against him, the Emperor seemed to see some sense at last and turned to the time-honoured way of raising cash – plundering the captive peoples of France and Spain.

He reserved the last of his Imperial revenues for one bizarre display in the Bay of Naples, where he moored 4,000 boats in a floating causeway – to give the lie to a prediction by a soothsayer who had told him as a boy that he had as much chance of becoming Emperor as crossing the bay and keeping his feet dry.

Caligula galloped across a wooden road of ships laid with turf, flanked with artificial gardens and mock taverns, to loot the city of Puteoli. Caligula then returned to Rome happy that he had proved the soothsayer wrong.

That night a storm wrecked almost half the ships still riding at anchor, and Caligula swore he would take his revenge on Neptune, the God of the Sea. The loss of the ships hasn't dampened his spirits enough to prevent him throwing a party for his favourite horse Incitatus, 'the swift', and presenting the animal with more classical paintings to join the collection already hanging on the walls of its marble bedroom. And Incitatus was 'promoted' from Senator to Consul of the Roman Empire.

Broke and desperate to recoup the cost of his Bay of Naples escapade, Caligula threw all caution to the wind. His guards rounded up ordinary citizens in the street and forced them to contribute every coin in their purses to the Emperor's treasury. Holding back a single coin could mean instant death.

When his loyal guards explained that they had even managed to rob the city's prostitutes of their meagre earnings, Caligula hit on his most obscene idea for raising even more revenue. At a family meeting in his palace, he raged at his sisters Agrippinilla and Lesbia: 'Everyone else in Rome has to work to support me, but I never see any money from you. Now it's your turn to work.'

By imperial decree, Caligula announced that his palace was to be opened as a brothel, with his sisters as prostitutes. Eminent senators were ordered to turn up at the enforced sex orgies and pay an entrance fee of 1,000 gold pieces. To the shame of the most noble men of the Senate, they were then summoned to return

Rome's enemies were equally capable of cunning cruelty. Mithridates was king of Pontus, a state on the Black Sea, now part of Turkey, for 59 years from 124 BC. In a surprise attack, he seized Syria and part of Asia Minor, taking thousands of Romans captive. Then he secretly instructed his generals to arrange a day of massacre. When the date arrived, 100,000 Roman men, woman and children were dragged out on the streets from their homes and slaughtered without mercy.

to another series of orgies and to bring their wives and daughters as prostitutes to join Caligula's sisters.

When Rome had been bled almost dry, Caligula decided to look further afield and, to the relief of his countrymen, set out to plunder his way through the captured provinces of France and Germany. He sent word ahead to the military garrison commanders and provincial governers in France that he wanted all the richest men in their areas to be assembled in Lyons to meet him. Nervously the Roman administrators complied, fearing that Caligula might rob and kill the

The young Emperor Nero never looked like being a threat to his fellow Romans when he succeeded to the supreme title at the age of 17 on the death of his stepfather Claudius. A foppish, bloated young poet who also fancied himself to be a talented musician and gifted architect, he showed no inclination to follow his predecessors as a warrior and great general. In the 13 years of his reign, he liked to pick on imagined enemies he could easily crush.

In 64 AD, when Rome was devastated by a fire which burned for a week. It was rumoured that Nero had started the blaze himself to rebuild the city and practise his amateurish architectural skill. But, far from accepting any blame, Nero found the perfect scapegoat for the blaze. The Christian religion was claiming a growing number of converts in Rome and Nero delighted in dreaming up cruel and bizarre new tortures for them. Instead of 'noble' gladiatorial contests in the circuses, he fed Christians to the lions. The wide roads leading to the arenas were lined with crucified Christians, coated in tar and set alight to form avenues of glowing torches to lead the audiences to the spectacle.

The citizens of Rome revelled in such delights. It helped them overlook the fact that Nero had murdered his own mother and his wife. But they drew the line when they discovered that he had castrated a slave and 'married' him to live as man and wife. When he heard he had been declared a public enemy and ordered to be flogged to death, the whimpering emperor clumsily committed suicide by slitting his own throat. His conceited dying words: 'This is a terrible loss to the world of art.'

French noblemen and provoke another Gallic uprising. But the tortured mind of the Emperor had produced an outrageous compromise. The rich merchants were being offered the bargain of a lifetime, a chance to buy some of the 'treasures' of Caligula's palace at knock-down prices.

So began the weirdest 'auction' any of them had ever witnessed. Caligula himself did the bidding on behalf of his captive buyers, bidding merchant against merchant until he was satisfied he had taken every piece of gold from them. When his sales assistants, the Imperial Guard, passed out the merchandise to the baffled bidders, the French merchants found they had unwittingly paid thousands of pieces of gold for packages of cloth which contained only old sandals and mouldy pieces of cheese.

With another small fortune in running expenses, Caligula set off for the Rhine, vowing to exterminate his German enemies. In one small skirmish, his legions captured about 1,000 prisoners. Caligula picked out only 300 men from the dishevelled ranks and ordered the remainder to be lined up against a cliff, with a bald man at each end. Satisfied he had enough prisoners for a swaggering triumphal entry to Rome, he ordered his Legions: 'Kill every man from bald head to bald head.'

Then he set off for his last great 'battle'. Camping outside the port of Boulogne, he ordered his dispirited and nervous army to line up on the beaches. Roman archers formed ranks at the water's edge. Huge catapults and slings were dragged on to the sand dunes to support the infantrymen; massed troops of cavalry waited on the flanks. All eyes were set on the horizon, watching disbelievingly for the appearance of some distant enemy.

Then Caligula rode with imperial majesty into the shallow water. With blood-curdling oaths, he unsheathed his sword and swore revenge on the sea god Neptune who had wrecked his ships in the Bay of Naples. The soldiers watched in silence as Caligula slashed at the foam with his sword. Then he ordered the catapults to be fired into the sea. The infantry charged, trampling the waves. The archers shot their arrows at the breakers. The shallow waters were pierced with spears and the cavalry rode in and out of the surf, stabbing the seawater with their swords.

'Now for the plunder', shouted an overjoyed Caligula. And each man had to begin looting the sea – gathering piles of sea shells in their helmets.

It was too much. The mighty Roman army had been reduced to clowning for their insane Emperor.

As Caligula began the long march home, the long-overdue conspiracy to rid the empire of the bestial lunatic quickly gathered strength. When Caligula entered Rome, bringing the straggling German prisoners and a handful of Britons he had captured from a trading boat in Bologne, together with tons of sea shells, the Senate was seething and the Army close to revolt.

For the next month they plotted. They let the mad Emperor rant and rave and award himself great honours for his 'victories'. Caligula drew up plans for all the statues of the Gods in Rome to be beheaded and replaced with an image of his own head. He danced through his palace in silken women's clothes and carried on blatant love affairs with young men he selected to be his bed partners.

But his days were numbered.

There was no mass uprising to overthrow him, just the sudden anger of one old soldier who had reached the end of his tether.

To Cassius Chaerea, colonel of the Imperial Guard, was given the most menial task of tax collecting. As an honourable soldier, he was sworn to give total obedience to his Emperor, no matter what the provocation. But when Cassius was ordered to torture a young girl falsely accused of treachery, he broke down and wept at the girl's pain and innocent anguish. Word of the veteran soldier's tears reached Caligula and the Emperor began to taunt him with shouts of 'cry-baby'.

To make sure all of the Guard knew of his insults, he teased Cassius mercilessly each day when he issued the new password for the Guard. Cassius was given the password personally by Caligula and had to repeat it in turn to each of his junior officers. The passwords had always been stern military slogans like 'victory' and 'no surrender'. Cassius had to repeat a new series given to him by the mocking Emperor, slogans like 'perfume and powder' and 'kiss me soldier'.

Cassius's sense of honour finally outweighed loyalty to a madman. In January AD 41, he waited in the covered walkway which separated Caligula's palace from his private theatre and sent in word to the Emperor who was watching rehearsals for a new play a troupe of young Greek dancing boys had arrived to perform for him. The perverted Emperor couldn't wait to meet the youngsters. He abandoned the audience and, as he hurried along the passageway, the old soldier Cassius stepped forward.

'I need the password for today, Emperor,' he told Caligula.

'Oh, yes,' said the leering Emperor. 'Let me see now. I think the password for today should be "old man's petticoat".'

It was to be his last insult. Cassius drew his sword and smashed Caligula to the ground.

With ten thrusts of the sword, from the skull to the groin, he ended the rule of the Divine Emperor Caligula. Seconds later he strode into the theatre and told the audience: 'The show is over, the Emperor is dead.'

There was a stunned silence. Then a roar of applause louder and more joyous than any heard during four years of depraved circuses and orgies of the wicked reign of Emperor Caligula.

Vlad the Impaler

If Dracula ever walked the earth as a creature of flesh and blood rather than a figure of fiction, then the person who deserved that terrible title was Vlad Tepes. But the legend of Count Dracula is a fairy-tale compared with the catalogue of terror, torture and sheer blood lust that marked the violent life of Tepes – otherwise known as Vlad the Impaler.

Vlad Tepes ruled over Walachia, now part of Romania, between 1456 and 1476. His father had been given the title 'Dracul' (meaning Dragon) because that creature was the emblem on his shield. His son, Vlad the Fifth, gave the title a new meaning by his habit of drinking the blood of his victims, of whom there was no shortage of supply. And his ingenuity in devising ever more horrible forms of death for his enemies was awesome.

On one occasion, he sat down to dinner surrounded by a large number of slowly dying victims. When one of his guests, sickened by the stench and the screams, made the mistake of complaining, Vlad had him impaled 'so that he could be above the smell'.

Twelve years of his reign were spent imprisoned in Hungary where, denied the pleasure of human victims, he pursued his solitary hours in the torture of animals.

Yet Vlad the Fifth was a hero in his own country, a brilliant general who ferociously set about putting an end to decades of internal strife and who then turned his attentions towards the Turks whose territorial ambitions were a perpetual threat to his borders. When the Turks sued for peace, Vlad summoned their envoys before him and had their hats and coats nailed to their bodies, using short nails to prolong their agonies.

Hungarian company director Sylvestre Matushka was tried in 1932 for causing the deaths of 22 people for his sexual gratification. He gained pleasure from witnessing catastrophe on a grand scale and sated his lust in a most extraordinary way. In August 1931 he set off an explosion that derailed an express train near Berlin, injuring 16 people. A month later he repeated the crime, blowing apart a Budapest-Vienna express and killing 22. He was apprehended while attempting a third explosion and jailed for life.

Impaling his victims on stakes was Vlad's favoured method of execution. He once triumphantly impaled 20,000 of his enemies. On another occasion, he partook of a hearty breakfast in a field of impaled peasants. He generally insisted that the stakes be made not too sharp – so that his victims would suffer more.

But there were other ways of avenging himself on those who offended him. A group of protesting peasants were invited to a feast at one of his homes, which was then locked and set on fire. He put down one rebellion by making it known that the bodies of plotters would be fed to the crabs, and the crabs then force-fed to their families – a threat he gleefully carried out. He also forced wives to eat the roasted bodies of their husbands and made parents cannibalize their children.

Vlad's excesses were not simply due to a cruel nature. He was a sadist who gained a perverted pleasure from his deeds and whose habit of drinking his victims' blood made him the model for the Dracula myth.

Vlad the Impaler's terrible rule came to an end in 1476 when he was killed in battle against the Turks – although it is believed that the blow that felled him came from one of his own lieutenants.

Gilles de Rais

While Vlad the Fifth was gaining infamy for his barbarity, a noble contemporary of his was gaining glory at the other end of Europe. Gilles de Rais (or de Retz) was a Marshal of France, one of the richest and bravest noblemen in the land, cultured, sophisticated and pious. His main claim to fame was that he fought alongside Joan of Arc. But his claim to infamy is in many ways more horrific than even Vlad's . . . for de Rais secretly tortured and killed hundreds of children to satisfy his craving for the shedding of blood.

Born in 1404, de Rais married into an equally noble family at the age of 16. He owned five vast estates, had a private chapel that required the attendance of 30 canons and was so esteemed in the eyes of the court that he was appointed to the post of Marshal so that he could personally crown King Charles VII of France. Of proud and muscular bearing, he was a brilliant warrior, being instrumental in securing Charles's victories over the English. He rode alongside Joan of Arc and was followed by a personal retinue of 200 knights.

Yet for all those glittering prizes, de Rais maintained a sick and savage secret. He was guilty of what a contemporary described as 'that which the most monstrously depraved imagination could never have conceived.'

He is said to have sadistically tortured and murdered between 140 and 800 children. Obsessed with the letting of blood, he would order his servants to stab his young victims in their jugular vein so that the blood would spurt over him. He was alleged to have sat on one dying boy while drinking his blood.

Ten years after Joan of Arc's trial for heresy, de Rais was charged with the same offence after he attacked a priest. Haughtily refuting that accusation, he was then charged with murder. In the words of his ecclesiastical accusers, he was a 'heretic, sorcerer, sodomite, invocator of evil spirits, diviner, killer of innocents, apostate from the faith, idolator.'

There was good reason for the Church to have fabricated the case against de Rais. He was a secular challenge to their power over the king and his court, and if found guilty the Church stood to seize his lands. No effort was spared in preparing the most damning case: de Rais's servants were tortured until adequate evidence was given against their master.

De Rais himself was probably not tortured. Yet he made a full and ready confession – not only to the murder of 140 children, of which he was charged, but to the murder of 'at least 800.'

Two rational reasons were given for this slaughter. The first was the influence on him of a book, an illustrated copy of *Lives of the Caesars* by Suetonius, which included graphic descriptions of the mad Emperor Caligula's sadistic excesses. The second was the approach of an Italian alchemist, Francisco Prelati, who promised the secret of turning iron into gold by black magic rites and sacrifices. But the real reason for the mass killings de Rais perpetrated could only have been what we now know as paedophilia and sadism – both carried out on a scale probably unequalled before or since.

Predictably, de Rais was found guilty and in a show of public contrition and humility begged forgiveness from the parents of the children he admitted slaughtering. Like Joan of Arc before him, he was sentenced to death by fire. But as an act of 'mercy' for not recanting his confession, he was first garrotted to death before being thrown on the flames on 26 October, 1440.

A mass murderer who was never caught, and whose reign of terror ended as suddenly and mysteriously as it had begun, stalked the streets of Cleveland, Ohio, between 1935 and 1938. Known as 'The Mad Butcher of Kingsbury Run,' he killed more than 12 men and women, chopping up the bodies into small pieces and leaving them in neat piles in alleys and on wasteland. Sometimes the victims, usually vagrants, would have parts of other corpses mixed in to the grisly pie. Few of the victims' heads were ever found – and the identity of the killer remains a mystery.

The Beane Family: the Ghouls of Galloway

Human monsters who practise vampirism or cannibalism are a vile but fortunately rare breed. Yet there is one case where such beings have not only worked as a team but as an entire clan. They were the notorious Beane family of Galloway, Scotland, made up of Sawney Beane and his wife, their eight sons, six daughters, 18 grandsons and 14 granddaughters.

Sawney (known as 'Sandy') Beane was the vagabond son of a road-mender and ditch-digger who lived near Edinburgh in the late fourteenth century. Driven out of town because of his n'er-do-well ways, Sawney fled with his young mistress to the rugged west coast of Scotland, where he settled in a cave and began to raise a family on the proceeds of sheep stealing and robbing travellers.

Their home provided a safe haven for their nefarious activities since its precise location was not known outside the family and because its entrance was blocked by the tide most of the time. But by 1435, at which time the Beane clan had increased by incestuous union to 48 members, the authorities were forced to act.

An entire tract of Galloway was prey to the ravages of the Beanes. And it was not just money, animals or property that travellers risked losing . . . it was their lives and bodies. For the evil clan had turned to cannibalism as the easiest and most satisfying way of both disposing of their victims and feeding their family.

James I of Scotland issued orders that the scourge of Galloway be ended and personally took charge of the force he assembled to clean up the coast. On the first foray of this policing operation, Beane's Gang was caught in the act. They were surprised while attacking a man and his wife and fled, leaving the woman's disembowelled body on the roadside.

With the help of dogs, the king's men tracked the Beanes to their lair. Inside the cave they found a charnel-house far exceeding in horror their worst nightmares. There were bundles of stolen clothes, saddles, food and valuables. There were animal carcasses. But in addition there were human corpses, both male and female, some dried, some smoked, some pickled and some salted. They hung, dismembered or still whole, from the damp roof of the cave.

All 48 Beanes were captured and taken to Leith where, after a show trial, the men had their hands, feet and private parts severed. As they bled to death, the women were burned alive – savage justice for the murder of dozens, and possibly hundreds, of innocent victims who ended up as dinner for Sandy Beane's bestial family.

Kürten and Haarman: the German 'Vampire' Killers

The label 'vampire' conjures up visions of dark, misty forests and bleak castles. But one of the most famous vampires in history was no part of this ancient mythology. The scenes of his appalling crimes were in twentieth-century urban Germany. His name was Peter Kürten and because of his vile deeds he became known as 'the Vampire of Düsseldorf'.

Kürten was a brutal sadist who first practised his perversions as a child of nine while working for the local dog-catcher near his home-town of Cologne-Mulheim. The youngster loved to torture the animals he rounded up, eventually progressing from dogs to pigs, sheep and goats. He was drawn hypnotically to the sight of blood and loved nothing better than to chop the head off a goose or swan and gorge himself on the blood that spurted out. Gradually Kürten switched from animals to human victims.

As a boy, he drowned two playmates swimming in the Rhine but there deaths were clean, easy, almost mundane. As an adult, he sought excitement through theft, fraud, arson and the beating of prostitutes. But the thrills he experienced were not enough and he coolly planned the ultimate crime, premeditated murder.

Strangely for such a calculating fiend, his first attempt failed. He attacked a girl in a wooded park, leaving her for dead. The victim, however, recovered and crawled away, too ashamed ever to report the incident.

His next attempt was tragically successful. The victim was an eight-year-old girl whom he strangled and raped before cutting her throat. The murder took place in 1913 but it was 17 years before the full story was known . . . related by Kürten himself at his trial.

Without emotion, he told the court: 'I had been stealing, especially from bars and inns where the owners lived on the floors above. In a room above an inn at Cologne-Mulheim I discovered a child asleep. I seized her head and strangled her for about a minute and a half. She woke up and struggled but lost consciousness.

'I had a small, sharp penknife with me and I held the child's head and cut her throat. I heard the blood spurt and drip on the floor. The whole thing lasted about three minutes, then I locked the door and went home to Düsseldorf.'

The following day, Kürten returned to the scene of the crime, sitting at a cafe opposite the bar where the girl had been murdered. 'People were talking about it all around me,' he said. 'It did me good.'

There was a tragic sequel to this murder, of which Kürten must have been fully aware. The butchered girl's uncle became prime suspect in the case. He was arrested and tried for murder. After a shameful trial, the poor man was acquitted but the stigma of the accusation haunted him until his premature death two or three years later.

Meanwhile, Peter Kürten, who had been called up for service in 1914, deserted within days and spent most of World War One in jail. Even when freed, he turned again to crime and was imprisoned for fraud. Finally released in 1921, he seemed to make a concerted effort to attain respectability. He got married, albeit to an ex-prostitute, gave up crime and took a job in a factory. He dressed smartly, spoke courteously and was well liked by his neighbours.

In 1925 the monster reverted to form. He employed prostitutes and beat them within an inch of their lives. Then he began attacking complete strangers in the street, mesmerized by the sight of their blood.

Kürten's savagery became uncontrollable in 1929. He accosted two sisters, aged 14 and five, as they walked home from a fair, strangled both and cut their throats. Within 24 hours, he pounced on a housemaid and stabbed her repeatedly in an uncontrollable frenzy until the blade of his knife broke off in her back. The girl's screams alerted passers-by who arrived in time to save her life but not to catch her attacker.

The city of Düsseldorf was by now in a state of panic. Police had a file of more than 50 attacks they believed had been committed by the man referred to as 'The Vampire'. But there was no suspect, no evidence, no link between the horrified victims and the quiet, self-controlled murderer.

Then, in 1930, the police were led literally to Kürten's door. A young country girl, newly arrived at Düsseldorf's main railway station, was being pestered by a stranger who promised to direct her to a cheap hotel. Just as the man's advances became frighteningly persistent, a second man arrived on the scene and intervened. As the first offender skulked away the 'rescuer' introduced himself – as Peter Kürten.

The girl was invited to recover from her ordeal with a meal at Kürten's home, after which he walked with her into the city's Grafenburg Woods and viciously assaulted her. Just as she was about to pass out, Kürten did what he had never done before . . . he allowed his victim to go free. He asked her if she could remember where he lived and, after naively accepting her assurance that she could not, he escorted her to a public thoroughfare and walked calmly away.

Incredibly, perhaps through a sense of shame, the girl did not go to the police,

At the same period that Fritz Haarmann was butchering innocents in Hanover, another German, the landlord of a rooming house in Munsterberg, Silesia, was also killing vagrants. Cannibalistic Karl Denke disposed of more than a dozen men and women, pickling their bodies for later consumption. Denke, seemingly a deeply religious man who played the organ at his local church, hanged himself in prison awaiting trial.

and the Vampire of Düsseldorf might even then have escaped capture except for an extraordinary coincidence. The young girl wrote of the incident to a friend but incorrectly addressed the letter. A postal official who opened it to seek the sender's address could not contain his curiosity and read the account of the attack. He immediately called in the police.

Detectives found the girl and made her retrace her steps to Kürten's home. There, they spotted Kürten but he had seen them first and fled through the streets. Under threat of capture, the killer turned to his unsuspecting wife. He met her in a restaurant where she worked and over double helpings of lunch, he confessed to her, in a matter-of-fact way, his many crimes. His disgusted wife arranged a further secret meeting but instead went to the police, who lay in wait for Kürten at the rendezvous.

In court, 47-year-old Kürten was as cool as ever. He horrified judge and jury by the calm, clinical manner in which he related in sickening detail the long catalogue of his crimes. He told how he had strangled, stabbed or clubbed to death his innocent victims and had then drunk the blood from one person's slashed throat, from another's wounded forehead and from another's half-severed hand.

His own defence counsel called him 'the king of sexual delinquents; uniting nearly all perversions in one person; killing men, women, children and animals – killing anything he found.' His lawyer was making a plea for a ruling of insanity, but to no avail.

Kürten was sentenced to die by guillotine and on the morning of his death, 1 July, 1932, he ate a hearty meal twice over, then told a prison doctor of his last hope . . . to experience what he described as 'the pleasure to end all pleasure'. It was, said Kürten, 'that after my head has been chopped off I will still be able to hear, at least for a moment, the sound of my own blood gushing from the stump of my neck'.

It is incredible that two 'vampire' killers could turn up in the same country in the same period. Yet while 'the Düsseldorf Vampire', Peter Kürten, was beginning to gain infamy for his deeds, another brutal monster was coming to the end of his reign of terror. He was Fritz Haarmann, 'the Hanover Vampire'.

At the end of World War One, Haarmann, then aged 39, emerged from a five-year jail sentence for theft and returned to his home town of Hanover to try to scrape together a living in the chaos of post-war Germany. The business he chose was as a purveyor of meats, pies and second-hand clothes in a poor area of the city. He prospered because of the cheap and simple source of his raw materials . . . murdered young men and boys.

Haarmann spent his evenings and nights prowling Hanover's railway stations and back alleys to seek out the human flotsam sleeping rough there. He would offer those who were jobless or homeless the chance of free food, lodging and companionship. In return, they would be sexually abused and often murdered. Their bodies would be butchered, their clothes sold and their flesh put into Haarmann's tasty pies.

The method of murder gave rise to Haarmann's sobriquet as 'Vampire of Hanover' – he would kill his victims by biting through their throats.

Incredibly, police and voluntary workers, who must certainly have suspected Haarmann, not only turned a blind eye to his nefarious activities but actively encouraged him. He became a police informer, passing on details of suspicious newcomers to town, of planned crimes and of hidden loot. So close was his relationship with the police that when in 1918 the parents of one 17-year-old boy reported their son missing after being seen in Haarmann's company, the ensuing search of the killer's room was no more than cursory. The murderer was later to boast at his trial: 'When the police examined my room, the head of the boy was lying in newspaper behind the oven.'

The following year Fritz Haarmann met the accomplice who was to speed up the 'production line' at his cooked meats plant. His name was Hans Gans; He was just 20 but was already a heartless, vicious thug whose job it was to pick out the victims ready for the executioner. Together, they began disposing of boys and young men at a prodigious rate.

Hanover had by now gained an unenviable reputation as the city where people could vanish from the streets without trace while the police were apparently powerless to act. In fact, the police could have acted and saved many lives, but they found Haarmann's information so helpful that they effectively gave him immunity. They even failed to respond to complaints about the one-way traffic of boys into Haarmann's rooms, the buckets of blood carried out and the bloodied clothes and suspect meat (labelled as pork) which he was selling.

Eventually, the discovery of two human skulls, one of a youngster, on the bank of the River Leine forced police to act. They searched the riverside and discovered more human remains. Boys playing nearby found a sack packed with human organs. And the dredging of the river bed raised more than 500 human bones. Haarmann's blood-spattered apartments and workshops were raided.

In December 1924 Haarmann and Gans went on trial. 'How many victims did you kill?' asked the prosecutor. Haarmann replied: 'It might be 30, it might be 40, I can't remember the exact number.' Asked how he had killed his victims, Haarmann replied dispassionately: 'I bit them through their throats'.

While Hans Gans received a life sentence (of which he subsequently served only 12 years) the Vampire of Hanover was predictably sentenced to death, having been found sane and entirely responsible for his bloody deeds. Before being beheaded, he declared: 'I will go to my execution as if it were a wedding.'

Herman Mudgett and the Chicago 'Torture Castle'

If there were a league table of mass killers, the name of Herman Webster Mudgett would be high on the list. He is reckoned to have murdered at least 200 victims – mainly young ladies – for the sheer pleasure of cutting up their bodies.

Mudgett researched his dreadful pastime at America's Ann Arbor medical school. An expert in acid burns, he boosted his student allowance by body snatching. He would steal corpses, render them unrecognizable, then claim on life insurance policies he had previously taken out under fictitious names. He got away with several of these frauds before a nightwatchman caught him removing a female corpse and the errant student fled.

Mudgett next turned up in Chicago where, under the alias 'Dr H. H. Holmes', he ran a respectable pharmacy without a hint of scandal. So successful was he that in 1890 he bought a vacant lot and set about building a grand house.

But this was no ordinary home. It contained a maze of secret passages, trap doors, chutes, dungeons and shafts. Suspicion was averted during the construction of what later became known as the 'Torture Castle' by the expedient of hiring a different builder for each small section of the house.

The house was finished in time for the great Chicago Exposition of 1893 when the city filled with visitors, many of whom were to be Mudgett's prey. He lured girls and young ladies to his 'castle' where he attempted to seduce them before drugging them. They were then popped into one of the empty shafts that ran through the building. The hapless girls would come round only to find themselves trapped behind a glass panel in an airtight death chamber into which would be pumped lethal gas.

The bodies would be sent down a chute to the basement which contained vast vats of acid and lime and, in the centre of the room, a dissecting table. Here Mudgett would cut up the corpses, removing particular organs which took his fancy and disposing of the rest in the vats.

Mudgett later admitted to having murdered 200 girls during the Chicago Exposition alone, and the orgy of bloodletting might have continued for much longer but for the phoney doctor's greed. He had murdered two visiting Texan sisters and, rather than quietly dispose of their remains, he set fire to the house in an attempt to gain the insurance money and make good his escape from Chicago.

The insurance company refused to pay and the police began an investigation into the blaze. Strangely, the police work was not pursued vigorously enough to produce any evidence of Mudgett's bloody activities – but the killer did not know this, and he fled.

This time he went south to Texas, where he traced relatives of the sisters he had so clumsily murdered. Having ingratiated himself with them, he tried to swindle them out of a $60,000 fortune. They were suspicious so Mudgett again took to the road, this time on a stolen horse. Police caught up with him in Missouri, where, using the name H. M. Howard, he was charged with a further fraud attempt. With the help of a crooked lawyer, he was granted bail – and promptly absconded.

Mudgett next turned up in Philadelphia where an associate in crime had been operating insurance frauds at the mass killer's behest. In an apparent accident one day in 1894, this co-conspirator blew himself up. In fact, he had been murdered by Mudgett who ran off to Toronto with his victim's wife and their three children. Their young bodies were later found in the basements of two rented houses.

It was not any of his many murders that finally brought Mudgett to justice but the jumping of bail in Missouri and the theft of a horse, a capital offence in Texas at that time. Detectives traced Mudgett through his aged mother who was happy to give them the whereabouts of the son of whom she was so proud.

The mass killer was arrested with his mistress in Boston and was charged with horse stealing and fraud. It was only at this stage that police searched the burned-out Chicago Torture Castle. They pieced together the remains of 200 corpses. Mudgett confessed to the murders of all of them. He was hanged on 7 May, 1896.

The Marquis de Sade

When police raided the house of 'Moors Murderers' Ian Brady and Myra Hindley in 1965, they found, along with the remains of one of their victims, the collected works of the Marquis de Sade. De Sade and Adolf Hitler's *Mein Kampf* were read as 'Bibles' in the killers' household. Although Hitler's philosophy is political and de Sade's sexual, both are in their own way equally dangerous. Both are able to snare the weak-minded. Both can turn mild men and women into monsters.

De Sade's distorted view of life, morality and sexual fulfilment is flaunted in books like *Justine*, *Juliette*, *Philosophy In The Bedroom* and *120 Days Of Sodom.* Stories of sexual deviation are told with relish. The extent of the perversions are limited only by de Sade's imagination – and that is considerable.

The man who gave his name to sadism was born Donatien Alphonse François De Sade on 2 June, 1740 in pre-Revolutionary Paris, which was a hotbed of vice and corruption. Related to the royal house of Condé, his father was a court diplomat and his mother a lady-in-waiting to the Princesse de Condé. Educated by his uncle, the Abbé de Sade of Ebreuil, he grew up good-looking, wealthy and spoilt. By the age of 18 he had experimented in every form of sexual adventure he could devise. But it was not enough. His over-fertile imagination began to invent new and terrible perversions to fuel his fantasies. The principal tenet of his philosophy was that the finest form of sexual pleasure is achieved through cruelty and pain.

De Sade served in the army during the Seven Years' War, leaving in 1763 and marrying the daughter of a judge. But within a month he was having an affair with an actress known as La Beauvoisin and was inviting prostitutes into the marital home at Arceuil. There he put his sadistic theories into practice with numerous victims, many of them strangely willing to subject themselves to his cruel whims. But some complained about their sexual abuse and de Sade was ordered to be detained in jail at Vincennes.

Within weeks he was freed and, despite having fathered two sons and a daughter by his long-suffering wife, he returned to his old ways. This time, his activities created a national scandal. In 1768 he hired a Paris prostitute called Rose Keller whom he locked up and tortured to such a degree that she complained to the authorities. De Sade was sent to jail in Lyons.

Possibly because of his family connections, he again secured an early release and in 1772 moved to Marseilles where in the busy port his pockmarked valet,

Latour, found for him a ready supply of prostitutes. But, as ever, his sensual experimentation was his undoing. De Sade fed the girls sweetmeats laced with various supposed aphrodisiacs. The girls were sick, believed they had been poisoned and complained to the police. The marquis and Latour fled.

At Aix, master and servant were sentenced to death in their absence and were executed 'in effigy'. The fugitives were finally captured and thrown into the fortress of Miolans. But de Sade still seemed to have the ability to get out of prison as easily he had got himself in. He escaped and hid away with his wife at their château. By now she too was debauched, both were in debt and further trouble with the authorities was inevitable. His wife became an enthusiastic partner in his perversions and when a new scandal broke involving young boys, both husband and wife fled.

The Marquise de Sade sought refuge in a convent while her husband bolted to Italy with his latest mistress – his wife's own sister, the Canoness de Launay. A year later, in 1777, they foolishly risked returning to France and de Sade was arrested in Paris. Thrown into the dungeons at Vincennes and then into the notorious Bastille, he suffered at the hands of harsh warders and fellow prisoners. The cruelty he had always been ready to mete out to others was now his lot.

His enforced isolation did, however, allow him to develop his blasphemous philosophy through his writing. In de Sade's eyes, there was no god but nature – and nature was not only the creator of beauty but also of destruction, through earthquake, flood, fire and tempest. Man's destiny, he believed, ran parallel with nature, and man's destructive impulses had to be obeyed in the same way as his more gentle ones were. So a truly 'complete' man should fulfil himself by becoming a monster.

De Sade propounded such lofty thinking as a camouflage for his real designs which are clear to see in books like his elegantly titled *120 Days Of Sodom* which was written in the Bastille on a single roll of paper about 12 metres (39 ft) long.

Ex-monk Joseph Vacher was committed to an asylum in 1893 and was released, supposedly cured, a year later at the age of 25. A series of mutilation murders followed across a wide area of south-east France. Vacher, who was leading the life of a tramp, killed and disembowelled eleven victims, five of them young boys. The 'French Ripper' was arrested in 1897 for an assault on a woman and was jailed for three months. In prison, he wrote to the authorities admitting all his crimes and asking to be sent back to the asylum. Judges accepted his confessions but not his plea to be treated as insane; he was executed in 1898.

The Marquis de Sade (based on contemporary descriptions)

He would probably have spent the rest of his days in prison but for a strange quirk of fate. In the chaos of the French Revolution – the Bastille itself was stormed on 14 July, 1789 – De Sade was freed.

Despite his aristocratic background, he became 'Citizen Sade', head of one of Paris's ruling revolutionary committees. As such, he managed to save his father-in-law from the guillotine – but only just escaped it himself. Strange as it may seem, 'Citizen Sade' began to deplore the unbridled brutality of France's new rulers and was accused of being a 'moderate'. He was sentenced to be guillotined but was overlooked in the prison line-up on his day of execution. The following day, Robespierre, hard-line leader of the revolutionary Convention, was overthrown and de Sade was safe once more.

In desperate poverty, he set up home with a young, widowed actress, Marie-Constance Quesnet, and wrote, among other books, *Justine* and *Juliette*. But it was these works that finally ended his freedom for ever. In 1801, on the basis of his writings, he was judged insane and locked up in Charenton asylum. Napoleon Bonaparte himself ordered that he never be released.

Visited by his actress mistress, he continued writing books and plays, which were performed by the asylum inmates. On 2 December, 1814 he died. His son visited Charenton, collected 13 years of his work and burned the lot.

A will was discovered. Written nine years previously, it instructed that his body was to be buried in the midst of a particular thicket on his old estate and the grave sown with acorns so that over the years it would be obliterated. He wrote: 'The traces of my grave must disappear from the face of the earth as I flatter myself that my memory will be effaced from the minds of men'. His wishes were ignored and de Sade the atheist was given a Christian burial, a stone cross being erected above his grave. Shortly afterwards the grave was broken into and the body stolen. The skull later came into the possession of a leading phrenologist who read de Sade's bumps and declared that he was a man of 'tender character and love of children'.

The contribution de Sade left to the world of literature is slight – but his contribution to criminality is considerable. The sickening philosophies he propounded have taken seed in the minds of the bad and the mad, the weak and the willing, murderers and mutilators from the beginning of the nineteenth century to the present day. Because he could so well express the fantasies of his own evil mind, others who followed him have been encouraged to act out their own. Indirectly, he may have been responsible for more murders than any other individual in peacetime history. The name of the Marquis de Sade is synonymous with evil.